COMMONIST TENDENCIES

Commonist Tendencies
Mutual Aid Beyond Communism

Jeff Shantz

punctum books * brooklyn, ny

Commonist Tendencies: Mutual Aid Beyond
Communism
© Jeff Shantz, 2013

First published in 2013 by
punctum books
Brooklyn, New York
http://punctumbooks.com

ISBN-13: 978-0615849782
ISBN-10: 0615849784

Library of Congress Cataloging Data is available
from the Library of Congress.

Cover Image: Brooklyn Bridge, August 2003,
Northeast Blackout

Facing-page drawing by Heather Masciandaro.

Contents

—~~—

01: BEYOND MOVEMENTS
TOWARD COMMONISM

As capitalist societies in the twenty-first century move from crisis to crisis, oppositional movements in the global North (which have been somewhat stymied (despite ephemeral manifestations like Occupy) are confronted with the pressing need to develop organizational infrastructures that might prepare the ground for a real, and durable, alternative. More and more, the need to develop shared infrastructural resources—what I have termed infrastructures of resistance (Shantz 2009)—becomes apparent. Ecological disasters (through crises of capital), economic crises, political austerity, and mass-produced fear and phobia all require organizational preparation—the common building of real world alternatives.

Confronted with these challenges, in the period of crisis and opportunity, movements of the global North have been largely perplexed by questions of how to advance, to build strength on a sustainable basis in a way that might pose real challenges to states and capital. Caught in cycles of repeatedly chasing after the next big momentary thing (Occupy, Idle No More protests in Canada, anti-pipelines demonstrations), they spin out largely symbolic manifestations or mobilizations that gain some attention but make few advances against states or capital. There are no guarantees that crisis will lead to success for movements seeking positive social change. At the same time, fascists, fundamentalists, and corporatists of various sorts find openings and opportunities, often supported by promotional capital (such as the Koch brothers) or governments seeking a social barrier against constructive resistance.

Movements of the Left, of various tendencies, have been searching for the momentum that was lost after September 11, 2001 shifted the terrain of opposition and contestation in much of the world. Energies have been turned toward media critique, civil liberties defense, anti-war opposition, and confronting the racist abuses of the war on terror. These are, of course, all important pursuits, but they are defensive rather than constructive.

The social movements of the global North have had particular difficulties intervening within relations of production. Indeed, this marks the critical challenge or barrier in their broader possibilities of development (Mezzadra and Roggero 2010). They have been largely separate from, and contributed little to, the workplace movements; this has been detrimental to both alternative globalization and workplace movements.

There is a need (as necessary now as ever) to think through what we—non-elite, exploited, oppressed—want, and how we might get it. There is an urgency to pursue constructive approaches to meet common needs. For many, the constructive vision and practice of meeting social needs (individual and collective) is expressed as commonism—an aspiration of mutual aid, sharing, and common good, or common wealth collectively determined and arrived at. According to autonomist theorist Nick Dyer-Witheford, the term commonsim is a useful way to discuss the goals and aspirations of oppositional movements, the movement of movements, because it returns to social struggle the emphasis on commonality—a common wealth—that has been lost in the histories of previous movements that subsumed the commons within mechanisms of state control, regulation, and accounting—namely communism. According to Dyer-Witheford:

> It is a popular term perhaps because it provides a way of talking about collective ownership without invoking a bad history—that is, without immediately conjuring up, and then explaining (away) 'communism', conventionally understood as a centralized command economy plus a repressive state. Though some will disagree, I think this distinction is valid; it is important to differentiate our goals and methods from those of past catastrophes, while resuming discussions of a society beyond capitalism. (2010, 106)

The reference to the commons means the collective lands and resources to which all have had access in meeting human social needs for almost all of human history on the planet. It speaks to the rootedness of humans as part of nature—an ecological as well as social consciousness. For commonists, the reference means even more specifically the common lands and resources that sustained peasant life in England in Western Europe historically, but which were stolen through violent (and legalized) practices of enclosure—in processes which Marx calls primitive accumulation—running from the late middle ages up through the present (Dyer-Witheford 2010, 106). Today, Dyer-Witheford speaks of "an ecological commons (of water, atmosphere, fisheries and forests); a social commons (of public provisions for welfare, health, education and so on); a networked commons (of access to the means of communication)" (2010, 106). These are the bases for sustaining human social life and development. They are in many cases, too, the outcomes of collective human labor, or collective human care (of land, water, education, and health).

Struggles over common lands and other common resources remain at the heart of vicious struggles waged in the twenty-first century. Contemporary neoliberalism operates according to a logic of new enclosures. The model of privatization of public services and institutions and the dismantling of social services pursues the enclosure of public resources—a portion of the surplus value produced by proletarians. It is an offensive against the para-commons, those collective resources wrestled from capital as part of previous rounds of social struggles and institutionalized (and controlled) within the auspices of the planner state. Neoliberalism seeks an extension of commodification into all spheres of social and ecological life.

The destruction of nature wipes out the common ground of human (and other) life. Indeed, the gross discrepancy between the privately held profit from resource extraction and industrial production (of and from nature)—a theft of and from the commons through enclosure/privatization—and the common eco/social sharing of the damage wrought by capitalist property and production—in the form of so-called externalities—shows starkly the conflict between commodity and commons.

In the current context, commonism, and the desire for commons, speaks to collective expressions against enclosure, now instituted as privatization, in various realms. While the central feature of capitalism is the commodity—a collectively produced good controlled for sale by private entities claiming ownership—the central feature of post-capitalist societies is the commons. For Dyer-Witheford:

> A commodity is a good produced for sale, a common is a good produced, or conserved, to be shared. The notion of a commodity, a good produced for sale, presupposes private owners between whom this exchange occurs. The notion of the common presupposes collectivities—associations and assemblies—within which sharing is organised. If capitalism presents itself as an immense heap of commodities, 'commonism' is a multiplication of commons. (2010, 106)

These counter-forces have always been in conflict throughout the history of capitalism's imposition. And this conflict has been engaged in the various spheres of human life, as mentioned above. Commonism, and commonist struggles, are expressed in intersections of sites of human activity and sustenance: ecological, social, and ideational. Examples of ecological commonism include conservation efforts, indigenous land reclamations and re-occupations (and blockades of development), and community gardens, to name only a few. Social commons include childcare networks, food and housing shares, factory occupations, and solidarity economics (including, but not limited to, community cooperatives). Ideational commons include creative commons, opens source software, and data liberation (such as Anonymous and Wikileaks).

Projects for common wealth (in labor and nature) confront class divisions within capitalism. The spread or circulation of commons provides a practical alternative to relations of capitalism and market logics. It hints at a new social order—commonist order. For Dyer-Witherford:

> We need to think in terms of the circulation of commons, of the interconnection and reinforcements between them. The ecological commons maintains the finite conditions necessary for both social and networked commons. A social commons, with a tendency towards a equitable distribution of wealth, preserves the ecological commons, both by eliminating the extremes of environmental destructiveness linked to extremes of wealth (SUVs, incessant air travel) and poverty (charcoal burning, deforestation for land) and by reducing dependence on 'trickle down' from unconstrained economic growth. Social commons also create the conditions for the network commons, by providing the context of basic health, security and education within which people can access new and old media. A network commons in turn circulates infor-

> mation about the condition of both ecological and
> social commons (monitoring global environmental
> conditions, tracking epidemics, enabling exchanges be-
> tween health workers, labour activists or disaster relief
> teams). Networks also provide the channels for
> planning ecological and social commons—organizing
> them, resolving problems, considering alternative pro-
> posals. They act as the fabric of the association that is
> the *sine qua non* of any of the other commons. (2010,
> 109–110)

This becomes procreative, or constructive. It provides a
spreading base for eco-social development beyond state
capitalist control. It also moves movements from momentary spectacles or defensive stances or reactive "fightbacks."
Commonism affirms and asserts different ways of doing
things, of living, of interacting.

There is, in the current commonist movements, "an
insurrection of subjectivities at the level of the common"
that breaks from both liberal individualism and socialist
collectivism (Mezzadra and Roggero 2010, 35). Conven-
tional relations of political belonging (individual/state, citi-
zen/nation) are broken. According to Mezzadra and Roggero:

> Instead there materialises a process of singular-
> isation in the common; or rather, in the conflict
> there is created that 'common place' that does not
> demand the sacrifice of the exploited singularities of
> which living labour is composed today. (2010, 35)

This is a commons marked by the ecological values of unity
in diversity. In practice it expressed tendencies of autonomy and solidarity.

There are strivings to develop new infrastructures for
shared social life, seeking a commons together. A mutual
aid—or solidarity—economy (which is after all commo-

nism itself) is at its base a way of producing, exchanging, and consuming values (produced directly by the people involved). It is the material base of social change. The mutual aid economy is a means of satisfying personal needs as well as collective welfare.

Acts of commonism are practiced by millions around the globe in solidarity economies based on cooperative labor and gift exchanges. These acts are what might be termed self-valorizing. Rather than producing and exchanging values for the benefit of capital (as surplus value or profit), these acts produce and circulate values for the benefit of those who produce them and their communities.

1.1: OF BLACKOUTS AND COMMONIST TENDENCIES

Living examples of the memory of the commons rising up "spontaneously" out of social conditions within capitalism are perhaps most readily or regularly observed under conditions of immediate need or emergency, as in times of natural disaster and/or economic crisis, during periods of revolutionary upheaval, or during mass events (such as festivals).

Many, perhaps most, of us who are caught up in the assembly line of daily life under industrial capitalism wonder, sometimes out loud, what would happen if the rat race suddenly, unexpectedly came to a grinding halt, all of the gears immobilized. What if someone just up and pulled the plug?

On Thursday, August 14, 2003 I found out, quite literally, as the streetcar I was riding home from work came to an immediate stop and all the lights went out. Not just the streetcar lights. Traffic lights, storefronts, and indeed every light for as far as I could see in every direction I looked.

While we didn't realize it at that moment, my fellow commuters and I were stranded right in the middle of the largest blackout in North American history. The power outage affected almost 50 million people across the northeastern United States from New York to Detroit and into the Canadian province of Ontario.

For many of the three million or so inhabitants of Canada's most populace city, the first response to the situation was confusion mixed with a dose of panic. In the post-9/11 world, people have come to expect the worst. A few rumours began to circulate. Another terrorist attack? Surely not on Canadian soil. We're peacekeepers aren't we? Who hates Canadians?

This could have gone very badly. Fear, frustration and a catalytic paranoia might have stoked the worst of those sentiments that often bubble over during even the regular daily urban grind. Road rage times three million.

Almost immediately, however, something incredible, beautiful even, began to happen. People, complete strangers, started talking with each other. Residents came down from their high-rise apartments, leaving concrete bunkers behind. Workers downed their tools and left their workplaces. The streets filled. And as people told stories and made jokes to pass the time, shared their concerns and offered possible answers, a certain joyfulness and good humour came over a city notorious among Canadians for its button-down lack of humour.

Even as word began to filter through that this was a blackout, a historic blackout, people let worries subside as they turned their thoughts towards making the best of the situation. And even more than that, planning ways to actually enjoy it. People brought down boxes and bags of thawing foods. Barbeques were rolled out of garages or carried down from fourteenth floor balconies. Tempting aromas filled the air. Food was shared freely. Given by people who really couldn't afford to give. "You're hungry after a long walk home. Come and eat." Musical instruments of all sorts appeared (Who would have guessed that so many musicians live here on our block. On every block).

An amazing jam session bringing together the myriad musical styles in this most multicultural of cities: country infused with reggae infused with folk infused with soukous. Singing, dancing, eating went on throughout the night. Never had the city, Toronto-the-sedate, seemed so alive.

"I had never even spoken with my neighbours until the blackout." This sentiment was repeated over and over again on each street I came to. And oh how people talked. Much has been made, quite rightly I think, over the decline of civic discourse recently. Bureaucratic, distant and alienating government and corporate structures leave masses of people with no sense of access, engagement, or effectiveness regarding social and political institutions and decision-making processes. The decline of public spaces for discussion, the agora of old, impelled by the rampant ethos of privatization, is a profoundly troubling characteristic of contemporary urban life. It is reflected at its most surface level in the low (and consistently decreasing) turnout for elections at all levels from municipal to federal. Yet, the blackout changed this, if only momentarily, as people took over the streets, their streets, and turned them into open "town hall" meetings. The return of the agora. And despite the dismissive portraits of "the public" offered by commentators of the left and right alike, as an apathetic, uniformed mass, people spoke confidently, insightfully and indeed incisively about their concerns for the future of the city, the province and the country.

This being a blackout, after all, much attention was given to the energy appetites of modern industrialism. The blackout made clear, both during street debates and in letters to the editor which followed, that many people were aware of the massive wastage of resources related specifically to corporate profit-making. And they were angry about it. Many pointed out the fact that the first day after the power came back on empty Bay Street (Canada's Wall Street) office towers were fully lit up. Numerous letters to the editor and calls to television and radio stations expressed disapproval over the use of energy to light up advertising signs and storefront displays. Energy directed to such useless ends is strictly a product of competition. And for the first time in a long time a very critical public discussion was taking place regarding such wasteful practices.

People noted that the historic blackout was only the most recent in a series of energy fiascoes that have stricken parts of North America as neo-liberal governments deregulate the industry and privatize power-generating facilities. Some reminded us that blackouts and brownouts have become a regular feature of profit-seeking energy provision in California since the industry was deregulated there.

Some long overdue recognition was given to environmentalists' calls for alternative energy sources and small-scale neighbourhood generators to replace energy megaprojects. Suggestions about how to take control of power away from governments and corporations and develop community control began to creep into public discussions, if only as a whisper.

Estimates of the economic cost of the blackout reach upwards of $5 billion. This says nothing about the lost incomes of workers whose workplaces were closed or operating in reduced capacities. The provincial government declared a state of emergency and told only essential workers to report for work. Yet for many, this was not felt as an emergency. It was felt as a break. Some time away from the daily grind that leaves us too tired, miserable, or harried to even enjoy a chat, a song, or a beer with our neighbours. Many expressed a certain disappointment when the lights came on again. "Aww, back to work I guess."

The word "blackout" is used to conjour visions of disorder, chaos, and disruption. We've all seen enough images or heard nasty stories from New York in 1977 or elsewhere to expect the worst. Partly, authorities want to maintain this sense of impending anarchy. "That's why we need the cops. People can't be trusted to look after themselves."

But of course we can, and in 2003 we did. Despite the cynics, the old and partly forgotten notion of mutual aid is alive and well, even in the cutthroat world of neo-liberal globalization (a world, remember, where Maggie Thatcher told us there is no society, only self-interested individuals). Many significant public engagements took place as a direct result of the blackout. Most importantly was the (re)emergence of community and solidarity in neighbourhoods across the city. Neighbours who had never so much as spoken to each other joined together to hold apartment and street parties. People improvised large-scale meals out of food that might otherwise have spoiled and fed entire streets. This was a glimpse of citizenship from below and even mainstream commentators remarked on how well people got by without businesses and the state.

A year later many were suggesting that we do it all over again. A commemoration of the blackout. Street festivals instead of work. Somebody pull the plug.

As Hartung explained, such moments are characterized by their brevity: "Traditional structure (form) is absent or in disarray and social order takes on a different content. The order experienced and created by the participants is situated in a fleeting social anti-structure" (1983, 90). Commonists work to extend mutual aid relations until they make up the bulk of social life.

Commonism is about developing ways in which people enable themselves to take control of their lives and participate meaningfully in the decision-making processes that affect us, whether around education, housing, work, or food. Commonists note that changes in the structure of work (notably in so-called lean production, flexibilization, and the institutionalization of precarious labor) have stolen people's time away from the family along with the time that might otherwise be devoted to activities in the community (Ward and Goodway 2003, 107). In response, people feel a pressing need to find ways to escape the capitalist law of value, to pursue their own values rather than to produce value for capital. This is the real significance of commonist do-it-ourselves activity and the reason that I would suggest such activities have radical, if overlooked implications for anti-capitalist struggles.

1.2: MOVEMENT NOMADS

There is a built-in defeatism to social movements in the global North. This built-in defeatism of movements (as distinct separates outside of everyday social relations) as "movements" is expressed in the glorification of movement (flow, action) itself (and specific forms of movement such as street manifestations). This reflects lowered aspirations within detached activist circles that are not connected with the needs of communities or even a sense of what basic successes or victories might look like. As activist collective The Free Association puts it, in rather depressing terms: "Or more prosaically *all* the movements can *ever* get from 'winning' is more movement" (2010, 104, emphasis added). Even the notion of victory or winning is denigrated. Unfortunately, they couch even this limited vision in terms of protest movements such as street demonstrations. In their view, "that's why we keep getting drawn back to counter-summit mobilizations like Heiligendamm: they are one of the places where the movement of movements can break the limits of its formation and ask its own questions" (2010, 104). Yet, in reality the counter-summits in no way break the limits of movement formation; rather, they are those limits. They express the very ground of its formation and reveal the limited horizons of its vision. Even more, these are largely spaces established, directed, and certainly policed by states and capital. They are not spaces of self-determination or broken limits. (They are, in fact, largely composed of limits.) Movements are always asking questions. Less often do they offer meaningful answers to communities in struggle.

Influential post-communist theorists like John Holloway embrace the rapture of movement expressionism. Holloway emphasizes the movement as a scream, as an exhilarating act of hurling ourselves against the world of capital. This is an exciting metaphor, one that plays upon the desire to expunge our frustrations with capitalist existence in a moment of emotional release—anti-capitalism as primal scream therapy.

But our movements are more, and hopefully more meaningful. They are made up of quiet moments of reconnecting, of building, of restoring, of constructing. More than a hurling against the walls, they are a shoulder to the wheel. They are a building of commons. In these moments they are more quiet than a scream. They are more about digging and planting than throwing or ramming. More prosaic than poetic. But, at the same time, they are all the more inspiring for it, because this gives them a chance to survive, to actually win.

Too many activists and their theorists romanticize movement, flight, flow. They disregard, despise, or denigrate building, constructing, producing (sneering about productivism). They resent the stability of structures. The rootless class, they resent rootedness. They shun the unromantic work of sustaining infrastructures. For Holloway: "Institutions, however, anti-institutional, seek to freeze the flow of time" (2010, 9). But do they? Or do they provide the refueling stations, the care centers? The homes and shelters. The spaces of security and sustenance. Fundamentally, these are precisely the places of connection. The very resources of sustenance and renewal (if not flow or nomadism).

This is not daring enough for the eternally restless. For Holloway, "taking the world into our own hands, assuming our own power-to, means that we try to swim (or skate or fly) without holding on to the edge for security. Perhaps we cannot live with such intensity, perhaps we need to rest from our moments of excess" (2010, 9). Further, he writes, "Hope moves faster than either perception or thought"

(2010, 9). But these are exactly what contemporary movements require, and perhaps lack, in relation to hope.

The movements in the global North put a lot of time and energy into imaginings of their becoming. Yet what they are becoming, what they are most proficient at becoming, is a subculture. Indeed, this is what they have become. The focus on creating a new "us" is emblematic of the subcultural splinter. It tends to be viewed as entry into the club, as markers of belonging.

Counter-summit actions and street protests, expressions of "activism," are privileged over everyday life (which is too boring or stifling or oppressive). The familiar forms of activism are said to "have proved essential" in helping the movements (subcultures) postpone capture. In any event, for The Free Association, "We can never entirely evade capture" (2010, 103).

Everyday life, and organizing within everyday struggles of life, makes seeing dynamics of change more difficult. Things "move" more slowly and work requires greater patience in workplace and community struggles. The nomad activists desire more for their desires: "Summit protests can shatter this everyday equilibrium and make the intensive realm spring to life. We can see commodities for what they are—dead. We get a sense that this is *real*, this is *life*" (The Free Association 2010, 103). "Spectacular eruptions" are supposedly required (The Free Association 2010, 103). This is the inversion—the movement uptake of the spectacle. The real is only observable, or recognizable, in (or as) spectacle.

Again, the everyday living of life, caring for families, supporting neighbors, changing daily structures daily, for the vast majority of the world's people is not quite real. It is certainly not as real as the exciting, exhilarating, lives of the protesters in the streets demonstrating their more exalted *real* life.

Yet the thrilling immediacy of the street eruptions quickly subsides, leaving little of real gain in its wake. As

Esteva suggests, "Rebellions are like volcanoes, mowing down everything before them. But they're also ephemeral; they may leave lasting marks, like lava beds, but they die down as quickly as they catch fire. They go out" (2010, 28). Real opposition to states and capital requires more than momentary joy. It requires foundations and infrastructures that contribute to significant advances while maintaining a basis for ongoing struggles.

As Mezzadra and Roggero suggest, "Even if the dissolution of the movement into thousands of tiny trickles, for example in Italy, has generated a certain identitarian retrritorialisation of different militant groups, we must not make the opposite mistake of being blinded by an aestheticised imaginary of deterritorialisation or a chimera-like nomadism that is incapable of becoming constituent power" (2010, 32). The contemporary movements require "common forms of organization and praxis" in order to "become trigger, engine and catalyst of the struggles of living labour today, the principle of a new conflictuality and a political practice beyond the simultaneously manifest and unsolved crisis of representation" (Mezzadra and Roggero 2010, 32). Precarity marks conditions of commonality in the current crisis state context. The counter-summit approach is not sufficient for further developing and empowering the conflicts over crisis and precarity.

Social relations are not fundamentally challenged at counter-summit demonstrations. Rather, they are reinforced and perhaps re-extended (in acts of repression and criminalization and the moralizing against "direct action" or militancy that comes, often most aggressively, from the Left itself). New worlds are not created despite the romantic fantasies of counter-summit protesters and their commentators (or cheerleaders). The work needed to re-store commons, as basis for survival and further struggle, is work of a different order.

There is a famous phrase attributed to the Zapatistas. It is expressed as follows: "Walking, we ask questions." It speaks to the desire for movement, but the continuation of critical inquiry along the way. The contemporary movements must proceed from a space of politicization to a space of organization in order to find radical answers rather than merely posing radical questions (Mezzadra and Roggero 2010).

1.3: COMMON PRACTICES?

New movements and new directions in organizing have common concerns but not common solutions, as Holloway points out (2010, 8). There are, too, common needs and common desires. These are desires and needs that have arisen along with capitalism; indeed, they are produced by it. These include needs for sustenance, for food, for shelter, for community. This is a desire for communion with nature and our fellows—for the commons.

Re-appropriating the commons is a struggle to stop the externalization of power, as Holloway puts it, to overcome alienation. For Holloway: "Power is indeed outside us, but our struggle is to dissolve the externality of power, to re-appropriate the world as ours. Or better: our struggle is to stop externalizing our power to stop alienating the world from ourselves" (2010, 8). Constructive approaches to (re)-build the commons halt the externalization of power while asserting collective capacities for the positive revision of social relations.

The experiences of the movements create common places through practice. And these hint beyond traditional institutions. Movements must pose a non-state public sphere, a commons. This becomes a key challenge for movements beyond capitalism. As Mezzadra and Roggero ask: "How can the changes form a sediment, how can power relations be affected, how can the opening and development of a constitutive space, a common, be secured? In other words, how can one employ the relations of power without 'taking power' (2010, 36)? This is the concern that has been at the forefront of anarchist theorizing and organizing.

Classical anarchist theorist Peter Kropotkin notes that the state, the formalized rule of dominant minorities over subordinate majorities, is "but one of the forms of social life" (1970, 131). For anarchists, people are quite capable of developing forms of order to meet specific needs and desires. As anarchist sociologist Colin Ward suggests, "given a common need, a collection of people will . . . by improvisation and experiment, evolve order out of the situation—this order being more durable and more closely related to their needs than any kind of order external authority could provide" (1973, 28). Order, thus arrived at, is also preferable for anarchists since it is not ossified and extended, often by force, to situations and contexts different than those from which it emerged, and for which it may not be suited. On the contrary, this order is flexible and evolving, giving way to other agreements and forms of order where necessary, depending on peoples' needs and the circumstances confronting them.

Even more, as many recent anarchist writings suggest, the potential for resistance can be found anywhere in the relations (and struggles) of everyday life. If power is exercised everywhere, it might give rise to resistance everywhere, though not, of course, to the same degree in all places. Contemporary anarchists point out that a survey of the social landscape of capitalist society reveals many collectivities and shared practices that are anarchist in practice if not in ideology:

> Examples include the leaderless small groups developed by radical feminists, coops, clinics, learning networks, media collectives, direct action organizations; the spontaneous groupings that occur in response to disasters, strikes, revolutions and emergencies; community-controlled daycare centers; neighborhood groups; tenant and workplace organizing; and so on. (Ehrlich et al. 1996, 18)

While these are obviously not strictly anarchist (or anti-statist or anti-capitalist) groupings, they operate to provide examples of mutual aid and non-hierarchical and non-authoritarian modes of living that carry the memory of the commons within them. Often the practices are, in fact, essential for people's day-to-day survival under the crisis states of capitalism. Colin Ward notes that, "the only thing that makes life possible for millions in the United States are its non-capitalist elements . . . . Huge areas of life in the United States, and everywhere else, are built around voluntary and mutual aid organizations" (Ward, qtd. in Ward and Goodway 2003, 105). Indeed, mutualist practices in everyday life have always provided fundamental supports for people within capitalist relations. The challenge remains to extend these practices so that they usurp the commodity formations of capital.

Ward suggests that, in this sense, anarchism, "far from being a speculative vision of a future society . . . is a description of a mode of human organization, rooted in the experience of everyday life, which operates side by side with, and in spite of, the dominant authoritarian trends of our society" (Ward 1973, 11). As David Graeber argues, the examples of viable anarchism are almost endless. These include a wide variety of organizational forms, from a volunteer fire brigade to the postal service, as long as they are not hierarchically imposed by some external authority (Graeber 2004).

What becomes key in the present period is "the capacity of the movements themselves to create their own institutions that—rather than stifle their growth—secure their reproduction, their development. Their capacity, to say it once more, to assert themselves within a common space" (Mezzadra and Roggero 2010, 33). This is a real move past the politics of demand. Rather than pursue demands (requesting something from someone outside of us, someone who is opposed to us) we create the world we desire. We build the future in the present (Shantz 2008). In this we assert our own productive power—which is always our greatest power—the very power that capital derives its vast wealth from. This, after all, is all we have ever had. We must use it for our own ends, for our own value. It is self-valorizing rather than valorizing for capital. In commonism, we re-appropriate our own productive power, taking it back as our own. We refuse to project our power onto an externality only to have it presented as a power over us.

As Mance concludes: "Our everyday practices must be guided by principles of solidarity, and our choices must be in agreement with the world we want to build. For that, we must strengthen the circuits of solidarity economy" (2010, 73). This is counter to a politics of demand. It is, again, a productive power—a self-valorizing power. It is expansive. It also propels and is propelled by further developments of infrastructures of resistance. As Dyer-Witheford suggests:

> This is a concept of the common that is not defensive, not limited to fending off the depredations of capital on ever-diminishing collective space. Rather it is aggressive and expansive: proliferating, self-strength-ening and diversifying. It is also a concept of hetero-geneous collectivity, built from multiple forms of a shared logic, a commons of singularities. We can talk of common earth, a common wealth and common net-works; or of commons of land (in its broadest sense, comprising the biosphere), labour (in its broadest sense, comprising reproductive and productive work) and language (in its broadest sense, comprising all means of information, communication and knowledge exchange. It is through the linkages and bootstrapped expansions of these commons that commonism emer-ges. (2010, 110–111)

Commonists suggest: "As the Zapatistas put it, to change the world is very difficult, if not impossible. A more prag-matic attitude demands the construction of a new world.

That's what we are now trying to do, as if we had already won" (Esteva 2010, 28). Commonists might argue along with the anarchist Paul Goodman who wrote during the social struggles of the 1960s:

> Suppose you had the revolution you are talking and dreaming about. Suppose your side had won, and you had the kind of society you wanted. How would you live, you personally, in that society? Start living that way now! Whatever you would do then, do it now. When you run up against obstacles, people, or things that won't let you live that way, then begin to think about how to get over or around or under that obstacle, or how to push it out of the way, and your politics will be concrete and practical. (quoted in Esteva 2010, 28)

For Goodman, whose writings greatly influenced the 1960s New Left and counterculture, what might be called commonist practices serve as necessary bases for "drawing the line" against the authoritarian and oppressive forces in society. Anarchism, in Goodman's view, was never oriented primarily toward some glorious future; it involved also the preservation of past freedoms and previous libertarian traditions of social interaction—experiences of the commons. As anarchist historian Peter Marshall argues: "A free society cannot be the substitution of a 'new order' for the old order; it is the extension of spheres of free action until they make up most of the social life" (1992, 598). Radical thinking will always be important, Goodman argued, in order to open the imagination to new social possibilities, but the contemporary anarchist would also need to be a conservator of society's benevolent and mutualist tendencies.

The key question is, once again, organization—infrastructure. Whether posed in terms of solidarity economics, positive welfare, cooperative labor, or especifismo, there are initiatives and engagements around the world involving millions of people striving to break the logics of capitalist production and exchange (especially of labor) in a durable and lasting way. These millions are striving to (re)create a commons.

These are not the usual suspects of alternative globalization movements or anti-summit protests. These are not the self-styled "activists" of street demonstrations and "campaigns." Indeed, most probably view such activists as a separate social category or strata, and look upon their campaigns with some skepticism (where they pay them any attention at all).

The mutual economies express the desires to collectively meet needs at individual and communal levels. These are desires for sustenance as well as liberation—for freedom from the imposition of forced labor under conditions of capitalist production. As Mance suggests, within solidarity economics:

> They work and consume in order to produce for their own and other people's welfare, rather than for profit. In solidarity economy what matters is creating satisfactory economic conditions for all people. This means assuring individual and collective freedoms, generating work and income, abolishing all forms of exploitation, domination and exclusion, and protecting ecosystems as well as promoting sustainable development. (2010, 67)

Worker-managed production efforts are exchanged in solidarity trade practices: shops, international fair trade systems, local trade fairs, and online exchange systems. As the commons products spread, new opportunities emerge. For Mance,

> This in turn enabled consumers to replace the products and services they bought from capitalist enterprises with products and services produced within the solidarity economy, feeding back into a

system of promotion of welfare for workers and consumers, environmental protection and sustainable development. Technologies such as free software and organic agriculture began being employed, developed and shared across these networks. (2010, 67–68)

What is at stake is a reorganization of productive chains. It is a battle over the very heart of capitalist social relations. Commonism does not wait for a revolutionary moment. Nor does it primarily make demands upon instituted authorities. For Esteva,

> We cannot wait for world revolution to dissolve the new forms of corporate capital. But we can attempt to make them marginal to our lives and to create new kinds of social relations. After refusing to be reduced to commodities and forced into alienated labor, after losing all the jobs many of us had, we are celebrating the freedom to work and we are renovating our old traditions of direct, non-exploitative exchange. We are thus enclosing the enclosers. (2010, 29)

Commonists are not satisfied with simply protesting against capitalist society and centralized, hierarchical structures of power. Nor are they content to wait for a post-revolutionary utopian future. The "new world" must come now, from within the shell of the "old world." Commonists are not seeking simply to live in the shadows of the government or states; they seek their complete dissolution. To develop the skills and resources that might contribute to this, commonists create counter-organizations and develop relations of production and exchange that foreshadow the structures of the future society in the here and now of everyday life.

1.4: CONCLUSION

Along the way it is important for commonists to fend off manifestations of statism in their ranks. Even rather clearsighted commentators like Nick Dyer-Witheford suggest that commonist projects are better off with "protection, support and even initiation at a state level" (2010, 111). He even suggests commons as part of a circuit involving autonomous assemblies and government agencies. This is a retreat into social democracy or statist communism. It is a recipe for re-enclosure. It is a recipe for defeat. The histories of previous social democratic and communist politics show this forcefully.

In many ways the politics of the Zapatistas, Seattle (alternative globalization street demonstrations), and Occupy excite people because they express (in embodied form) responses, not only to capital but to the imaginal and material failures of approaches previously taken by the political Left—namely by various forms of communism. Movements of communism failed to defeat capitalism or to restore a commons. Their failures were along negative and positive lines.

There is now a need to get beyond the nostalgia of the past. To leave the Left behind. To squarely face what has been wrong. To stare down the ghosts that haunt us. We must consign communism to the crypt of the Left. This means abandoning its organizational forms, namely the party and the vanguard cadre.

We must also resist the claims, quite often made, that the new form of cooperation for the movements of resistance is the network. As Mezzadra and Roggero suggest: "The problem is that the network model itself is being practised today in a rather 'weak' form, rather than treating it as a powerful—and reproducible—organizational principle, capable of giving a political answer to the dissolution of the vanguard faction in the living body of struggles" (2010, 32).

Cultural manifestations and transformations can be important, but they are not enough to effect lasting change or to build a base for future struggles. In order to build a commons, and a new world beyond capital, infrastructures of sustenance are needed. As Mance puts it: "The 'good fight' must be fought on the economic plane (not just in culture or politics). There is a revolution underway, but 'to be winning' means expanding and strengthening the collaborative processes that may form the base from which a possible post-capitalist society can emerge" (2010, 67). This emphasis on the collaborative base for sustainable movements to confront or move beyond capitalism has been missing from much of the social activity characterizing movements in the global North, movements which have almost exclusively prioritized symbolic or ephemeral street manifestations.

New struggles and new openings emerge. Recent struggles, especially those of migrant workers, show the strategic significance of conflicts over mobility and the control of mobility at all levels from local to global. This signifies "a historic phase in which mobility has become a decisive factor in the development of work, civil society, and forms of life" (Mezzadra and Roggero 2010, 31). This is a redefining and redeployment of class struggle at a transnational level.

A (re)turn to commonism expresses sustainable relationships between movements and everyday life. Movements of the Left over the last few decades in the global North have largely been separated from the social, operating rather as subcultural manifestations of social ephemera and marginality. The integral link that marked past movements, which has been lost in the present day Left of the global North, must be restored. Movements must give dedicated attention and effort to develop effective and durable approaches by which the gap between would-be revolutionary movements and everyday movements can be overcome, the connection made, in the real world of everyday life and struggle.

Building alternatives to capital in a meaningful way that can support and sustain human social life and struggles requires, rather than special or unique "activist" cultural expressions, infrastructures of resistance. These infrastructures must be rooted in real social relations as part of struggles of everyday life (overwork, social care, community and family sustenance, and so on, in work-places, neighborhoods, and homes). These are practical initiatives. As Mance suggests, hinting at the need for infrastructures of resistance,

> More than simply spreading information about proposals, and this acting on the level of ideological debate, it is necessary to operate on political and economic planes, putting some of the proposals into practice. In other words, our *daily economic practices* must be part of the work of transforming global economic structures. (2010, 67, emphasis added)

Building these daily economic practices, spreading them throughout the spheres of social life, is a tendency of commonism (built of many interlinked initiatives).

02: SOCIALIST TENDENCIES

Socialism, generally defined, refers to some type of collective ownership and control of a society's means of production, subsistence and exchange. Over time and in diverse contexts, the specific mechanisms of control and practices of collective decision-making have ranged from state control of the economy, as in numerous Soviet systems, to libertarian control through popular assemblies. Socialism, in its various manifestations, has served as one of the great mobilizing doctrines of modernity. Its political vision of radical democracy and egalitarianism served simultaneously as the specter haunting capitalist ruling classes and the tantalizing promise of a better world for poor and working classes.

While the term socialism emerged in the 1820s in France and England, proto-socialist tendencies and/or emphasis on common goods and equality can be found in some forms of Taoism, Plato's *Republic*, the Bible's "Sermon on the Mount," St. Thomas More's *Utopia* and millenarian movements of the Middle Ages. Groups such as the Levellers and Diggers during the English Civil War of the 1640s and the *sans culottes* of the French Revolution gave expression to ideas that are now identified as socialist. It should also be noted, however, that in Asia, Africa and the Americas, many of the indigenous or non-colonial societies were actually organized as socialist societies in which the necessities of life were shared within relatively egalitarian communities. Indeed, for most of human history, social life has been organized in a manner that could be termed socialistic or communistic.

The diverse strands of socialism have been divided over key issues of social organization and social change. Crucial differences have involved centralized versus decentralized governance, private versus collective or communal property, degrees of hierarchy and equality, revolutionary or evolutionary and reformist approaches to social change, and the place of the state in social change and the redistribution of social wealth.

2.1: UTOPIAN SOCIALISM

The earliest socialists presented their ideas as visions of future societies based on material equality, in which humans cooperated to meet human needs through relations of care and mutual aid. Typically, these social schemes envisioned a society in which states and private property were replaced by collective or mutual ownership and self-government (or anarchism). Early socialist theorists included Robert Owen, Charles Fourier, Louis Blanc, Alexander Herzen and Henri de Saint-Simon.

Because these perspectives were based on the creative desires of those who constructed them, rather than an assessment of social viability or a real consideration of the obstacles to be overcome in achieving the imagined social scheme, these early theories were sometimes identified as "utopian" socialisms.

Fourier foresaw a future society based on small, local, face-to-face communes or *phalansteries*, organized around the human desires of participants. These communes exhibited a desiring economy with basic, rather than complex, levels of social organization. The progressive factory owner Robert Owen envisioned a collectively run cooperative society based on workers' co-ops in which workers owned and controlled productive apparatuses and machinery, and made all decisions over production and exchange. He tried to bring these ideas to life through the experimental industrial community "Harmony."

Louis Blanc abhorred violent calls for revolutionary seizures of power. Instead, he suggested that a revolutionary regime might deploy democratic means while acting as a banker to the people, assisting associations of working people. Private property would eventually be excised from agriculture, trade and industry. Significantly, he argued that people be paid not according to the work they completed but according to the needs they expressed. This would provide the basic maxim, "from each according to their ability, to each according to their need," which formed the central tenet of communism (rather than mutualism or collectivism), both anarchist and Marxist.

Without doubt, the most influential early socialist was the French theorist Pierre-Joseph Proudhon. Proudhon, the first self-identified anarchist, advocated the free association of producers, including individual producers, as a replacement for the coercive state. People would organize their own affairs on the basis of personal contracts, which would be arranged on the basis of mutual gain and interest. These contracts were not permanent and participants could end them at any time that their concerns failed to be met. Such arrangements, for Proudhon, must be freely entered into and freely left. Unlike collectivists, Proudhon argued that individuals should own and control their means of production and the products of their own labours.

Early socialists foresaw socialism as the gradual outgrowth of human social development as people became more enlightened and the saw the "rightness" of the new social arrangements. Small, utopian communities or collectives would gradually spread as their ideas and ways of living became more appealing than the exploitation and inequalities which most people suffered under capitalism.

Despite the beauty and even brilliance of their ideas and

social visions, utopian socialists were largely ineffectual in realizing broad or lasting social change. Eventually, new forms of socialism emerged, critical of the gradual, evolutionary, utopian views of social change.

Forms of revolutionary socialism, and communism (both anarchist and Marxist), emerged, eventually gaining predominance within working class and radical movements. Early versions of revolutionary socialism tended to advocate armed insurrection by small, active bands of revolutionaries who would foment social change through acts of violence culminating in *coups d' etat*. The most popular of early revolutionary socialists was Louis-Auguste Blanqui. Blanqui upheld the Jacobin tradition of rule by terror and dictatorship. He advocated insurrectionary action and violent revolution to overthrow the ruling classes. Socialism would be established through a dictatorship that would suppress the former ruling classes and support working class social, economic, and political interests. Under communism, which he viewed as the highest level of human development, the aristocracy and capitalists would lose their civil rights. The state would be dissolved and replaced by a revolutionary apparatus committed to ongoing revolution. The standing army would be abolished and replaced by militias of the people. No mere theorist, Blanqui actively led numerous uprisings, generally without success.

2.2: MARXISM OR "SCIENTIFIC SOCIALISM"

Following the brutal suppression and repressive aftermath of the 1848 revolutions in Europe, social reformers developed a stark analysis of the prospects for socialism. During the revolutions in Germany, a new variant of organized socialism came to prominence, articulated most notably and forcefully in the *Manifesto of the Communist Party* by Karl Marx and Friedrich Engels. This so-called "scientific socialism," based on revolutionary communist principles, broke from utopian socialism and argued for socialists to concretely analyze relations of power in society, particularly authority and property—social relations—in developing a socialist outlook and strategies for social change. Most significantly, socialism could not be wished into being. Capital and the state would always violently oppose socialist projects. The basis of socialism was not good intentions or beautiful schemes, but the balance of social forces in society.

Marxism offered a theory of history—historical materialism based on social relations rather than the history of ideas—and a theory of society based on an analysis of shifting class relations. For Marxism, human social history has been marked by class struggle rather than consensus or peaceful evolution. Under capitalism the primary conflict is between the ruling bourgeoisie (the capitalist class of property owners), and the majority of society (the proletariat or working classes of people who owned nothing except their capacity to work). Scientific socialism argued that capitalism could only be overthrown through a violent revolution against the forces of the state and capital. A dictatorship of the proletariat or working class would be necessary to suppress forces of the former ruling classes, as the dictatorship of the bourgeoisie had violently suppressed the oppressed the working class under capitalism

Socialism was not the task of middle class social reformers or benevolent members of the ruling classes. Only the working class or proletariat, the majority of society, could undertake the needed revolutionary transformation that would usher in socialism or communism. Change would come on the basis of working class needs, as workers confronted the contradiction of collective production by the working class within a context of private ownership by the bourgeoisie. Revolution would see the working class institute collective ownership to match the reality of collective production. Because the proletariat constituted almost all of capitalist society, they represent, for Marxism, a "universal" class whose liberation will mean the liberation of all humanity and the end of oppression.

Most revolutionary socialists and Marxists have long maintained that one cannot properly understand, nor can one adequately address, inequality and injustice without linking it to deeper issues of class and exploitation underlying capitalist social relations. Class analysis recognizes that within capitalist societies the vast majority of people are separated from the means of producing their basic subsistence, including food, clothing, housing, and other necessities. This majority, the working class, must survive by selling their capacity to work to those capitalists who own and control productive resources and is therefore in a precarious socio-economic position. Thus, the material conditions enjoyed by a minority in capitalist societies are directly related to the material exclusion of the majority. Poverty is socially produced rather than resulting from characteristics of the individual.

As long as productive property, or what is sometimes referred to as the means of production, is privately controlled in hands of the few who make decisions about what will be produced, when, and by whom, leaving working people in a condition of having to sell their laboring capacity to these owners of capital, there will be inequality, injustice, and poverty. The negative features of private ownership and control are exacerbated by capitalist competition which, in the search of individual capitalists for competitive advantage against their challengers, leads to technological innovations, or labor-saving devices, that contribute to unemployment as well as the movement of production in search of cheaper labor. Because private ownership, competition, and production for profit are primary elements of capitalism, poverty is also produced as a regular feature of capitalism.

A class analysis of inequality leads to the conclusion that social reforms cannot end injustice within the context of a capitalist economy. As a result, proponents of class analysis advocate and work towards more radical and thorough, even revolutionary transformations of capitalist society, generally in the direction of a society organized on the basis of some form of socialist or communist social relations. In the most radical versions of class analyses of society, the only possible way to really reduce or eliminate poverty is to abolish capitalist social relations altogether.

2.3: ANARCHY IS ORDER

The strand of revolutionary socialism that gained prominence and a mass base within working class movements in the 19th century, and which challenged Marxism directly, was anarchism. The word "anarchy" comes from the ancient Greek word "anarchos" and means "without a ruler." While rulers, quite expectedly, claim that the end of rule will inevitably lead to a descent into chaos and turmoil, anarchists maintain that rule is unnecessary for the preservation of order. Rather than a descent into Hobbes's war of all against all, a society without government suggests to anarchists the very possibility for creative and peaceful human relations. Proudhon neatly summed up the anarchist position in his famous slogan: "Anarchy is Order."

Pierre-Joseph Proudhon, the first to call his social philosophy "anarchist," argued that vice and crime, rather than being the cause of social antagonisms and poverty as popularly believed, are caused by social antagonisms and poverty. He considered State order to be "artificial, contradictory and ineffective," thereby engendering "oppression, poverty and crime" (1969, 53). In his view, the constitution of societies under States was strictly anomalous. Furthermore, "public and international law, together with all the varieties of representative government, must likewise be false, since they are based upon the principle of individual ownership of property" (1969, 54). For Proudhon, jurisprudence, far from representing "codified reason," is nothing more than "simply a compilation of legal and official titles for robbery, that is for property" (1969, 54). Authority is incapable of serving as a proper basis for constituting social relations. The citizen must be governed by reason alone, and only those "unworthy and lacking in self-respect" would accept any rule beyond their own free will (1969, 94). In place of political institutions, Proudhon advocated economic organizations based upon principles of mutualism in labour and exchange, through co-operatives and "People's Banks," as a means towards that end. The consequences of this re-organization of social life include the limiting of constraint, the reduction of repressive methods, and the convergence of individual and collective interests. This Proudhon calls "the state of total liberty" or anarchy, and suggests that it is the only context in which "laws" operate spontaneously without invoking command and control.

Michael Bakunin, who popularized the term "anarchy" and whose work was instrumental in the early development of the anarchist movement, argues in his scattered writings that external legislation and authority "both tend toward the enslavement of society" (1974, 240). In his view, all civic and political organizations are founded upon violence exercised from the top downward as systematized exploitation. Any political law emerging from those organizations is an expression of privilege. Bakunin rejects all legislation, convinced that it must turn to the advantage of powerful minorities against the interests of subjected majorities. Laws, inasmuch as they impose an external will, must be despotic in character. For Bakunin, political rights and "democratic States" are flagrant contradictions in terms. States and laws only denote power and domination, presupposing inequality: "Where all govern, no one is governed, and the State as such does not exist. Where all equally enjoy human rights, all political rights automatically are dissolved" (Bakunin 1974, 240). Bakunin distinguishes between the authority of example and knowledge, "the influence of fact," and the authority of right. While he is willing to accept the former situationally and voluntarily, he rejects the latter unconditionally:

When it is a question of houses, canals, or railroads, I consult the authority of the architect or engineer . . . though always reserving my indisputable right of criticism and control . . . . Accordingly there is no fixed and constant authority, but a continual exchange of mutual, temporary, and, above all, voluntary authority and subordination. (Bakunin 1974, 253–254)

The influence of right, an official imposition, he terms a "falsehood and an oppression" which inevitably leads to absurdity (1974, 241). Like Proudhon, Bakunin envisions future social organizations as economic rather than political. He sees society as organized around free federations of producers, both rural and urban. Any co-ordination of efforts must be voluntary and reasoned.

Peter Kropotkin divided all laws into three main categories: protection of property, protection of persons and protection of government. Kropotkin saw that all laws and governments are the possession of privileged elites and serve only to maintain and enhance privilege, and he argued that most laws serve either to defend the appropriation of labour or to maintain the authority of the State. Speaking on the protection of property, Kropotkin noted that property laws are not made to guarantee producers the products of their labour but rather to justify the taking of a portion of the producer's product and placing it into the hands of a non-producer. For Kropotkin, it is precisely because this appropriation of labour (and its products) is a glaring injustice that "a whole arsenal of laws and a whole army of soldiers, policemen and judges are needed to maintain it" (1970, 213). In addition, many laws serve only to keep workers in positions subordinate to their employers. Other laws (those regarding taxes, duties, the organization of ministerial departments, the army and police) serve no other end than to "maintain, patch up, and develop the administrative machine," which is organized "almost entirely to protect the privileges of the possessing classes" (Kropotkin 1970, 214).

With regard to "crimes against persons," he viewed this as the most important category because it is the reason the law enjoys any amount of consideration and because it has the most prejudices associated with it. Kropotkin's response is twofold. First, because most crimes are crimes against property, their removal is predicated upon the disappearance of property itself. Second, punishment does not reduce crime. His reflections led him to conclude that not only is law useless, it is actually hurtful—engendering a "depravity of mind" through obedience, and stoking "evil passions" through the performance of atrocity. Because punishment does not reduce the amount of crime, Kropotkin also called for the abolition of prisons. The best available response, he argued, is sympathy.

Twentieth-century anarchists have developed these readings of State/society relations in more nuanced ways. Of much significance for contemporary anarchist analysis is the work of Gustav Landauer who, more than a half century before Foucault, offered a vision of power as de-centred and situationally enacted. Landauer conceptualized the State not as a fixed entity outside of extraneous to society but as specific relations between people dispersed throughout society.

2.4: ORGANIZATION

The task of socialists was to organize workers into groups or collectives to wage class struggle towards revolution. Socialists were understood as an active minority within the working class who worked to agitate amongst workers and spread socialist ideas more broadly.

Socialist political groups emerged in the 1830s and, from the start, a split emerged between those who emphasized organizing within political parties and those who advocated organizing within economic organizations centered around trades unions. Following the 1848 events, socialist movements began to develop mass support and participation from broad sections of the working class. Over the last decades of the 1800s, alliances between the political parties and union organizations developed.

The first major international alliance emerged in the form of the International Working Men's Association, or First International. Founded in London in 1864, with a conference addressed by Marx, the International would bring together socialist activists from most countries of Europe, anarchists, syndicalists, communists, revolutionists, and reformists alike. Most of the groups at the first conference were tiny—although spurred by revolutionary events in France and Germany and the presence of the International itself. The socialist organizations enjoyed rapid growth in numerous countries. From the start, internal conflicts and disagreements over strategies, tactics, and future directions racked the organization.

Foremost among these divergences was Michael Bakunin's famous disagreements with Marx over the role of the state in the transition to socialism. Bakunin's central conflict with Marx was related precisely to the former's conviction that an authoritarian revolutionary movement, as Marx espoused, would inevitably initiate an authoritarian society after the revolution. For Bakunin, if the new society was to be non-authoritarian then it could only be founded upon the experience of non-authoritarian social relations. The statement produced by Bakunin's supporters in the IWMA during his battle with Marx in 1871 asked: "How can you expect an egalitarian and free society to emerge from an authoritarian organization?" (Joll 1964, 216). This conviction was repeated a century later by participants in the Paris insurrection of 1968: "The revolutionary organization has to learn that it cannot combat alienation through alienated forms" (Marshall 1992, 658). For anarchists, because one cannot achieve freedom through authoritarian means, attempts to expose, subvert and, indeed, to abolish structures of domination should be pursued in ways, and using forms, that demonstrate in practical terms that those structures are not needed (see Graeber 2004, 7). Anarchists attempt to develop autono-

mous and egalitarian forms of self-government—a perspective that, for Marxists, returns them to the realm of the
utopian.

The libertarian section of the International arrayed
around Bakunin was expelled from the International at the
1872 Hague Congress. Behind Bakunin, they went on to
form the Anarchist International, the Jura Federation.
Anarcho-syndicalism would become the predominant form
of socialism in France, Spain, Italy, and Latin America
through the first half of the twentieth century, before
succumbing to forces of fascism and dictatorship.

2.5: Syndicalism

Syndicalism refers to diverse movements and perspectives
which take the collective self-organization and direct action of
the working class, both at the point of production and within
working class communities, as the basis not only for over-
coming capitalism but for organizing a new, egalitarian
society. While tracing its origins to the trade union movements of the nineteenth century, the term syndicalism comes
from the French word for unionism: *syndicalisme*. It has come
to signify a radical or revolutionary approach to labor
organizing, which seeks to overthrow the wage relationship,
capitalists, and class society rather than collectively bargain
workers' place within the wage relationship.

Historic anarcho-syndicalist campaigns have provided
significant evidence that class struggles entail more than
battles over corporatist concerns carried out at the level of the
factory. Syndicalist movements have displayed attitudes of
hostility towards the bureaucratic control of work, concerns
over local specificity, and techniques of spontaneous militancy and direct action. Syndicalist struggles have, in different
instances and over varied terrain, been articulated to engage
the broader manifestations of domination and control.
French revolutionary syndicalism placed an emphasis on
radical democracy. Within syndicalism, one can discern such

themes as consensus formation, participation of equals, decentralization, and autonomy.

Syndicalist theories of capitalist power place emphasis upon an alternative revolutionary worldview that emerges out of working-class experiences and offers a challenge to bourgeois morality. Fernand Pelloutier, an important syndicalist theorist whose works influenced Georges Sorel, argues that ideas, rather than economic processes, are the motive force in bringing about revolutionary transformation. Pelloutier vigorously attempted to come to terms with the problem of cultural domination as a basis for capitalist power. Reconstituting social relations, in Pelloutier's view, becomes possible when workers begin developing revolutionary identities through self-preparation and self-education, as the means for combatting capitalist culture. Thus, syndicalists have characteristically looked to labor unrest as an agency of social regeneration whereby workers challenge the cultural hegemony of class domination, e.g. deference to authority, acceptance of capitalist superiority, and dependence upon elites. Unlike versions of authoritarian communism, such as Marxism and Leninism, syndicalism understood the transformation of power not in terms of the replacement of one intellectual elite by another but as a process of diffusion spreading power out into the workers' own organizations. This displacement of power would originate in industry, as an egalitarian problematic, when workers came to question the status of their bosses. Towards that end, syndicalist movements have emphasized "life" and "action" against the severity of capitalist labor processes and corresponding cultural manifestations.

It might be argued that, far from being economistic, syndicalist movements are best understood as counter-cultural in character, more similar to contemporary new social movements than to movements of the traditional Left. Syndicalist themes such as autonomy, anti-hierarchy, and diffusion of power have echoes in sentiments of the new movements. This similarity is reflected not only in the syndicalist emphasis upon novel tactics such as direct action, consumer boycotts, or slowdowns. It also finds expression in the extreme contempt shown by syndicalists for the dominant radical traditions of its day, exemplified by Marxism and state socialism, and in syndicalist efforts to divorce activists from those traditions.

Syndicalist unions, as opposed to bureaucratic unions, sought the organization of workers from the bottom up. Their strategies rejected large strike funds, negotiations, written contracts, and the supposed autonomy of trades. Actions took the form of "guerilla tactics" including sabotage, slowdown, planned inefficiency, and passive resistance.

Perhaps the strongest and certainly the most enduring variant of syndicalism developed within anarchist movements in Spain and much of Latin America. Anarcho-syndicalism viewed the revolutionary self-organization of workers in radical opposition to capital, outside of not only union bureaucracies but outside of mainstream union frameworks themselves (limited as they were by collective bargaining over workers' contracts), as the means by which an anarchist society might be realized. Anarcho-syndicalism reached its highest level of popular involvement in Spain in the early decades of the twentieth century. The Confederation Nacional del Trabajo (CNT) played a major part in the Spanish Revolution and the resistance to the fascist regime of General Francisco Franco during the 1930s. The CNT was especially active in Barcelona during the revolution, running industries and providing social services in the region while organizing the armed resistance to fascist forces on the front lines.

Syndicalism also developed powerful movements in North America, most notably the Industrial Workers of the World (IWW or Wobblies), which was active in the US, Canada, and Mexico (especially in the early 1900s), and the One Big Union that organized the Winnipeg General Strike in 1919. Destroyed almost completely by the Red Scare of 1919, the IWW has enjoyed something of a resurgence in the twenty-first century, especially among precarious workers in service industries often unorganized by the declining mainstream industrial unions. IWW perspectives, with regard to capital, emphasize workers' abilities and encourage the self-determination of workers and the importance of self-directed initiatives against capital. The IWW asserts that workers must organize themselves to fight employers directly. The symbolic unity of the working class and its break from capital is stressed in the single qualification for Wobbly membership; the only restriction to membership in the IWW is that no employer can be a member.

A primarily intellectual version of syndicalism was developed by the social theorist Georges Sorel in the 1910-1920s in France. Revolutionary syndicalism, as this variant was known, saw working class direct action as the basis for a new society based on values of heroism and sacrifice, which stood counter to the apathy and social degeneracy of bourgeois society. Syndicalism, and worker direct action, stood also as a refutation of the rule of society by bureaucratic and technocratic professionals. For Sorel, the general strike was most important not as a practical approach to labor organizing but rather as a "revolutionary myth" that served to rouse the fighting spirits of the working class and provided them with an image of the power of their unity in struggle. The vitality of the general strike was not so much material as ideological.

Syndicalism has enjoyed a resurgence recently in many parts of the world as workers seek an alternative to mainstream unions that seem unwilling to fight against multinational corporations. Many workers, including younger workers and workers in small workplaces which are often overlooked by mainstream unions, have turned to syndicalist organizing.

2.6: SOCIAL DEMOCRACY

The Marxists eventually left the IWMA to the anarchists, and in 1893 met in Paris to found the Second International, or Socialist International. In reality, this was the social democratic international as it was dominated by formal socialist parties that sought, and increasingly gained, electoral success in those countries in which working people were allowed to vote. The theories of the Second International offered a revision of Marxist tenets, especially by arguing that socialism could be compatible with liberal democracy and social transformation, at least in advanced industrial capitalist countries, which might be effected through evolutionary, even electoral means. Social democratic versions of socialism, as represented by some labor parties, maintain that the negative characteristics of capitalism could be moderated through policies that, without infringing upon private ownership, could still make significant gains in reducing poverty or lessening the impact of poverty on people's lives. Important reformist social democratic parties included the SFIO, *Section de l'Internationale Ouvriere* in France, founded by noted theorists Jean Jaures and Leon Blum. In North America, Western Europe, Australia, and New Zealand, the main currents of socialism were organized around the mass parties of social democracy.

Social democracy, unlike revolutionary forms of socialism which it generally opposes, takes a gradualist approach to the development of socialism. For advocates of social democracy, socialism, especially within wealthier liberal democracies, can be achieved peacefully through electoral politics. Socialist parties, rather than being underground cadre groups, are structured as mass public parties organized towards the achievement of electoral success and participation within parliament. In practice, social democratic parties were often opponents of revolutionary communism, siding with the ruling classes in their own countries against communist political activists and organizers within working class institutions such as trade unions. Like the communists they opposed, social democrats also preferred hierarchically structured organizations and representational, rather than participatory, politics according to centralized party leadership and discipline.

During the 1890s, the Social Democratic Party (SPD) in Germany became the largest and most influential socialist party in Europe. Its leaders, including Eduard Bernstein and August Bebel, were identified as "revisionists" for their alteration, even abandonment, of Marxist revolutionary principles and advocacy of a parliamentary path to socialism. In their view, socialism could be entirely pursued through electoral and parliamentary means in countries with full franchise and liberal democratic governance. "Revisionist" and "revisionism" would become terms of disparagement for socialists over generations, expressing a sell-out of real socialist principles and a fatal compromise with capitalism. Over time, the SPD became more revisionist and conservative. During the 1910s and 1920s it played an active role in suppressing revolutionary working class uprisings in Germany and Austria. The SPD played a crucial role in crushing the uprisings of 1919, including the Munich Council Republic, allying itself with he proto-fascist *freikorps* militias. The SPD government arrested leading revolutionary socialists and communists, including Karl Liebknecht and Rosa Luxemburg. The crushing of the leftist movements during 1919 and 1920 is viewed as having set the stage for the rise of the Nazis in Germany.

2.7: BOLSHEVISM AND SOVIETISM

The strongest opposition to revisionism came from anarchists outside the Second International and from communists in countries in which liberal democracies were not established. Most significant among these were the Russian social democrats under Valdimir Ilyich Lenin. In particular, a formal split in 1903 saw the party divide between revolutionary (Bolshevik or majority) and reformist (Menshevik or minority) factions. Lenin's Bolshevik's echoed Blanqui in advocating a violent revolutionary path to communism. Key in this is the active involvement of a close cadre of committed and dedicated revolutionaries who would agitate and foment revolutionary organizations and practices within working class communities. These cadres would form the vanguard of the revolution, a necessary element in bringing the masses to revolutionary consciousness for Leninists. Lenin also advocated for a communist organizational model that was highly centralized within the Communist Party.

With the outbreak of World War I in 1914, the failings of social democracy were painfully put on display as the parties in Germany, France, and Britain succumbed to national chauvinism supporting the entry of "their" national states into war and thus sanctioning the slaughter of millions of working class people. Even some anarchists such as Kropotkin succumbed to chauvinism, arguing for the victory of French culture over the barbarism of Germany.

Among the clear-sighted was Lenin who called, from exile in Switzerland, for working class revolution in all combatant countries as a means to end the bourgeois war of imperialism and set in motion the shift to socialism. The 1917 Russian Revolution, which took Imperial Russia out of the war, confirmed Lenin's thesis. It also thrust the Bolshevik approach to revolution to the centre of world socialism, marginalizing anarchism and social democracy in many parts of the world for decades. Factions of almost every socialist party split to form Communist Parties on Lenin's vanguardist Bolshevik model. In 1919, Lenin initiated a new Third International, or Communist International, to bring together these Communist Parties.

Even early on the Bolshevik regime showed signs of the authoritarian dictatorship that Bakunin had warned socialists against during the First International. Alternative socialist parties, such as the peasant-dominated Socialist Revolutionaries and anarchist groups were criminalized, their members subjected to persecution, imprisonment and execution. Many fled the country as exiles, fleeing the very revolution they had played central roles in bringing about.

Early on, important anarchists like Alexander Berkman and Emma Goldman initially worked with the Bolsheviks, even translating Lenin's writings, before becoming profoundly disillusioned by the persecution of anarchists and the sacrifice of revolutionary aims to the self-interests of the party bureaucracy. The violent suppression of the Kronstadt rebellion and the state murder of the sailors and workers led Berkman and Goldman to conclude that the revolution was finished, killed by the dictatorship.

In 1929, Joseph Stalin came to power, shifting Bolshevik internationalism and solidarity towards a policy of national development or "socialism in one country." This shift was effected through a withdrawal of support from parties in other countries and the executions of leading Bolsheviks.

For many in poorer or "developing" countries, socialism, and especially the example of the Russian Revolution, offered a model for the coincidence of industrial/economic and governmental/political revolutions. This revolutionary model, in which a seizure of national power provided a lever for rapid industrialization, held great appeal throughout the twentieth century within numerous countries of the global south. As post-colonial governments looked for means by which to "catch up" with the industrial might of the former colonial powers, the approach of socialism, especially statist socialism, seemed to provide both a potentially effective political program and an ideological justification for statist reorganization of the economy and work.

In the context of the Soviet Union and communist China under Mao, socialism meant Stalinism and the centralized control of the economy and politics under the bureaucracy of the Communist Party. Thus, the meaning of socialism was taken very much away from its origins in visions of communal ownership, material equality, self-determination, and co-operative production.

Indeed, the extent to which Sovietism contradicted or

violated the aims and principles of historical socialism is perhaps best reflected in the violently authoritarian response to popular movements for workers' control and self-management, whether in the broad context of society or the much more limited context of the workplace. For many, this justification for the government suppression of popular assemblies, workers councils, and other forms of working class self-management was a violation of the most fundamental principles on which socialism stood. That such an inversion of socialism, from defense of the working-class against ruling elites to the legitimization of elite rule over the working class, could come from a government calling itself socialist led many to rethink the character of the Soviet-styled regimes and to seek out alternative, even non-Marxist, visions of socialism. Many gave up on socialism altogether.

The Soviet economies were still beholden to the law of value, only rather than being controlled by private capitalists, value under Soviet economies was held by the bureaucracy, which served as a form of monopoly capital. Competition for markets and exchange was still supreme, however, it was not the competition between individual firms, as in liberal capitalism, but rather the competition between the monopoly capital of various states, as between the Soviet Union and the U.S., for example.

2.8: FORGOTTEN TENDENCIES: MUTUALISM

The dominance of statist forms of communism have left many commonist tendencies overshadowed, marginalized, or obscured. Some have been nearly erased from histories of progressive radicalism. Mutualism is a social and economic theory, most often associated with anarchism, which traces its roots to the writings of Pierre-Joseph Proudhon. Mutualists follow Proudhon in envisioning future social organizations as economic rather than political. They see society as organized around free federations of producers, both rural and urban.

Any co-ordination of efforts must be voluntary and reasoned.

Mutualists differ from other anarchists, as well as from most communists and socialists, in allowing for the existence of private property and even money in a post-capitalist society. Mutualists are less concerned with private property than with the monopoly control of property by corporate interests backed by the state. They argue that a large proportion of the wealth created through social and technological development in a market economy becomes concentrated in the hands of monopolists by way of economic rents. This concentrated, unearned, and unproductive wealth is the primary casue of poverty in capitalist economies. Collecting private profit by restricting access to natural resources, upon which all depend for survival, amounts to a system of theft and slavery. This is made even worse given that productive activity, such as industrial works, were burdened by taxes while land values were not. Natural resources are the product of nature rather than human labor or initiative and, as such, should not provide the basis by which individuals acquire revenues. Nature, as the common heritage of all humanity, must be made a common property of society as a whole.

For mutualists, everyone is entitled to the products of their directly applied labor, through individually or collectively controlled means of production, and payment should reflect socially produced value. Mutualists advocate for a "free market" unsupported by the state force or laws that allow and protect concentrated wealth. This includes a labor market in which people choose, without coercion, to work for others, for themselves, or co-operatively. A mutual credit bank provided money to facilitate this scheme. Unlike communism, which advocates exchange on the basis of the maxim "from each according to ability, to each according to need," mutualism advocates trade on the basis of equivalent amounts of labor.

A distinction is sometimes drawn between individualist or philosophical anarchism, with its emphasis on individual liberty and personal transformation, and communist anarchism, with its emphasis on equality and collective mobilization for broad social change. Mutualism is often viewed as a mid-level perspective between these two approaches. Philosophical anarchism places greater emphasis on individual freedom to act unfettered by the constraints of social mores and norms. While placing less emphasis on the individual, and emphasizing co-operative labor, mutualism also differs from social anarchism in its distrust of large-scale social organization, especially the mass organizing for radical or revolutionary social change preferred by socialists and social anarchists.

Mutualists understand anarchism not as a revolutionary establishment of something new, a leap into the unknown, or as a break with the present. Rather, they regard anarchism as the realization of anti-authoritarian practices of mutual aid and solidarity that are already present in society, but which have been overshadowed by state authority. As Paul Goodman suggested, anarchism is the extension of spheres of freedom until they make up the majority of social life. Starting from this perspective, mutualists seek to develop non-authoritarian and non-hierarchical relations in the here-and-now of everyday life.

Mutualist anarchism, unlike that of anarchist communism, is based on gradual, non-violent rather than revolutionary social and cultural change. In place of force, Benjamin Tucker advocated the liberation of the individual's creative capacities. Tucker looked to gradual enlightenment through alternative institutions, schools, cooperative banks, and workers' associations as practical means to enact change. Social change, for Tucker, required personal transformation first and foremost, but at the same time, while rejecting force (which he termed domination), Tucker did assert the right of individuals and groups to defend themselves.

Proudhon's notions of People's Banks and local currencies have returned in the form of LETS (Local Exchange and Trade Systems). In North America, 19th Century mutualist communes, such as those of Benjamin Tucker, find echoes in the autonomous zones and squat communities of the present day.

Recent and contemporary theorists who present versions of mutualism include Paul Goodman, Colin Ward, Hakim Bey and Kevin Carson.

2.9: AND COMMUNALISM

Communalism refers to a range of diverse perspectives, theories, and movements in which social change is founded in the re-development of community, as a site of close, personal face-to-face relationships, in opposition to the anonymity and impersonal character of industrial capitalist society. One of the most influential early notions of communalism can be found in the works of the German sociologist Ferdinand Tonnies who presented the community as an alternative to the cold calculation of market-based society (*Gesellschaft*) that was replacing the close ties of rural life (*Gemeinschaft*).

The term became increasingly popular in the late-twentieth century, especially among progressive activists and leftists seeking an alternative discourse on communal societies beyond the discredited forms of authoritarian Communism, Marxism, Sovietism, and Leninism. It has become particularly popular among contemporary anarchists, notably those influenced by Murray Bookchin's writings on social ecology and libertarian municipalism. Bookchin saw communalism not only as the development of a new public sphere that might oppose the state and capital, but as an alternative to the anti-collectivist emphasis on individualism and personal autonomy in libertarianism and much of contemporary anarchism. For Bookchin, communalism offers the directly democratic and practicable aspect of anarchist politics, a means, in the here-and-now of existing social relations, by which alternatives to the impersonal capitalist market and the bureaucratic state management of society might be implemented. An initial step might be the development of federated neighbourhood assemblies as community decision-making bodies. This confederal structure of directly democratic assemblies, Bookchin calls libertarian municipalism.

For communalism, social life is organized primarily in small communes, in which community decisions are based on consensus and participatory democracy in face-to-face meetings involving all members. In place of a national state, a central decision-making body consisting of professional governors who decide for communities they do not belong to; under communalism, local communes come together in a confederal association of re-callable delegates to address issues of mutual interest and concern such as trade.

Communalist movements have included communal living arrangements in urban centers, "back-to-the land" movements such as the hippies of the 1960s, utopian communities such as New Lanark, and present-day land trusts in which property is owned collectivity.

Anarchists view communalist arrangements as a precursor to the large-scale transformation of society as the confederation of communes, the "commune of communes," comes to pose an alternative to the state for growing numbers of people. Eventually, having been rendered obsolete, the state will wither away.

03: COMMONIST TENDENCIES
MUTUAL AID, ANARCHY, AND COMMUNISM

Contemporary commonism finds perhaps its clearest precedents in the works of classical anarchist writers. For example, Pierre-Joseph Proudhon, the first to explicitly identify his theory as anarchist, sought the basis for social transformation through co-operative experiments such as workers' associations and the so-called People's Bank. Proudhon urged workers to emancipate themselves by constructing their own alternative economic institutions. Revolutionary anarchist Mikhail Bakunin, for his part, viewed trade unions not simply as economic institutions but as the "embryo of the administration of the future" and argued that workers should pursue co-operatives rather than strikes, constructive rather than reactive projects (Marshall 1992, 627). At the same time, recognizing the impossibility of competing with capitalist enterprises, he called for the pooling of all private property as the collective property of freely federated workers' associations. Ideas such as these would serve as the intellectual impetus for anarcho-syndicalism and its vision of the industrial syndicate as the seed of the future society.

Perhaps the most suggestive historical influences on commonism today are Peter Kropotkin's anarcho-communism and the libertarian socialism of Gustav Landauer. In *Mutual Aid*, Kropotkin documents the centrality of co-operation within animal and human groups and links

anarchist theory with everyday experience (1902). Kropotkin's definition suggests that anarchist society, fundamentally, "would represent an interwoven network, composed
of an infinite variety of groups and federations of all sizes
and degrees . . . temporary or more or less permanent . . .
for all possible purposes" (quoted in Ward and Goodway
2003, 94). Commonist styles of sociation and organization
express the persistence of supposedly archaic forms within the
(post-)modern context. They reveal the return of the
repressed in sociological types exemplary of "mechanical solidarity" and *Gemeinschaft*.

Perhaps the most interesting touchstone in the current re-
envisioning of anarchy has been the largely forgotten work of
Gustav Landauer, the most influential anarchist thinker in
Germany after the proto-anarchist Max Stirner. Inspired by
the works of the early sociologist Ferdinand Tönnies, Landauer identified himself as an "anarchist socialist" to dis-
tinguish himself from popular currents of Stirnerist egoism or
individualist anarchism. Drawing upon Tönnies' distinction
between *Gemeinschaft* (organic community) and *Gesellschaft*
(atomized society) and the ongoing conflict between these
within industrial capitalist societies, Landauer theorized the
rebirth of community from within the shell of statist and
capitalist society. Recognizing the persistence of *Gemeinschaft*
relations within modernist societies Landauer suggested that
the forms within which the new society would gestate were to
be the *bunde*: local, face-to-face associations. Like Proudhon
and Bakunin before him, Landauer advocated the formation
of producers' and consumers' cooperatives as a means for
restoring a commons as a basis for a post-capitalist community.

The anarchist-socialist community, for Landauer, is not
something that awaits a future revolution for its realization.
Rather it is the growing discovery of something already
present in current social relations: "This likeness, this equality
in inequality, this peculiar quality that binds people together,
this common spirit is an actual fact" (Marshall 1992, 411). In

as much as anarchism would involve revolution, this "revolution," for Landauer, would consist of elements of refusal in which individuals withdraw co-operation with existing state institutions and create their own positive alternatives:

> The state is a condition, a certain relationship among human beings, a mode of behaviour between them; we destroy it by contracting other relationships, by behaving differently toward one another . . . We are the state, and we shall continue to be the state until we have created the institutions that form a real community and society of men. (Marshall 1992, 411)

Landauer thus advocated the development of self-directed communities that would permit a break from institutions of state and capitalist authority. Revolution, reconceptualized by Landauer, was a gradual rejection of coercive social relations through the development of alternatives. This view of revolution as a process of constructing alternative forms of sociation—used as the model for a new society—is largely shared by contemporary anarchists.

> Revolution is a process, and even the eradication of coercive institutions will not automatically create a liberatory society. We create that society by building new institutions, by changing the character of our social relationships, by changing ourselves — and throughout that process by changing the distribution of power in society . . . . If we cannot begin this revolutionary project here and now, then we cannot make a revolution. (Ehrlich et al. 1996, 5)

In many of his writings, the anarcho-syndicalist Sam Dolgoff stresses the importance of this constructive approach to anarchism, rich in positive and practical ideas rather than reactive, momentary acts or negative impulses. Again, the means for a constructive anarchism are already available in currently existing social relations, even if these relations are overshadowed and limited by the authoritarian society that dominates them.

> The anarchist theoreticians limited themselves to suggest the utilization of all the useful organisms in the old society in order to reconstruct the new. They envisioned the generalization of practices and tendencies which are already in effect. The very fact that autonomy, decentralization and federalism are more practical alternatives to centralism and statism already presupposes that these vast organizational networks now performing the functions of society are prepared to replace the old bankrupt hyper-centralized administrations. That the "elements of the new society are already developing in the collapsing bourgeois society" (Marx) is a fundamental principle shared by all tendencies in the socialist movement. (Dolgoff 1979, 5)

If society really is "a vast interlocking network of cooperative labour" (Dolgoff 1979, 5), then those networks of cooperation will provide a good starting point, if only a starting point, in throwing off the restraints of coercion, authoritarianism, and exploitation. It is in the relations of cooperative labor, which encompasses millions of daily acts, that one can find the real basis for common social life. Without these networks, usually unrecognized and unpaid, society would collapse and survival for millions would be threatened.

> What is needed is emancipation from authoritarian institutions OVER society and authoritarianism WITHIN the organizations themselves. Above all, they must be infused revolutionary spirit and confidence in the creative capacities of the people. Kropotkin in working out the sociology of anarchism, has opened an

avenue of fruitful research which has been largely neglected by social scientists busily engaged in mapping out new areas for state control. (Dolgoff 1979, 5)

A beginning step in these processes of emancipation is the abolition of the wage system and the distribution of goods and services according to the old communist principle, "from each according to ability, to each according to need":

Libertarian Communism is the organization of society without the State and without capitalist property relations. To establish Libertarian Communism it will not be necessary to invent artificial forms of organization. The new society will emerge from the "shell of the old." The elements of the future society are already planted in the existing order. They are the syndicate (union) and the Free Commune (sometimes called the 'free municipality') which are old, deeply rooted, non-Statist popular institutions spontaneously organized and embracing all towns and villages in urban and in rural areas. The Free Commune is ideally suited to cope successfully with the problems of social and economic life in libertarian communities. Within the Free Commune there is also room for cooperative groups and other associations, as well as individuals to meet their own needs (providing, of course, that they do not employ hired labor for wages). The terms 'Libertarian' and 'Communism' denote the fusion of two inseparable concepts, the individual pre-requisites for the Free Society: COLLECTIVE AND INDIVID-UAL LIBERTY. (Dolgoff 1979, 6)

Of course, experiences of both the syndicate and the free commune have been greatly diminished and eroded, if not entirely eliminated, over centuries of state capitalist imposition. The social consequences of this historical reality have been addressed by the anarchist Paul Goodman in rather poignant terms: "The pathos of oppressed people, however, is that, if they break free, they don't know what to do. Not having been autonomous, they don't know what it's like, and before they learn, they have new managers who are not in a hurry to abdicate" (quoted in Ward 2004, 69). That means that people have to construct approximations in which the social relations of a commons (present and future) can be learned, nurtured, and practiced.

This is part of the impetus behind the creation of cooperatives, "free schools," industrial unions and community gardens. These places in which the life of the free commune, buried beneath the detritus of authoritarian systems, can be glimpsed again, if only in a tentative or partial form. For Dolgoff,

> Anarchism envisions a flexible, pluralist society where all the needs of mankind would be supplied by an infinite variety of voluntary associations. The world is honeycombed with affinity groups from chess clubs to anarchist propaganda groups. They are formed, dissolved and reconstituted according to the fluctuating whims and fancies of the individual adherents. It is precisely because they "reflect individual preferences" that such groups are the lifeblood of the free society. (1979, 8)

In his discussion of the US labor movement, "The American Labor Movement: A New Beginning," Dolgoff reminds readers that the labor movement once put a great deal of energy into building more permanent forms of common institutions. An expanding variety of mutual aid functions were provided through unions in the early days of labor.

> They created a network of cooperative institutions of all kinds: schools, summer camps for children and adults, homes for the aged, health and cultural centers, insurance plans, technical education, housing, credit assoc-

iations, et cetera. All these, and many other essential services were provided by the people themselves, long before the government monopolized social services wasting untold billions on a top-heavy bureaucratic parasitical apparatus; long before the labor movement was corrupted by "business unionism." (1980, 31)

That Dolgoff learned these often forgotten or over-looked lessons from a critical engagement with the labor movement is significant. As a militant anarchist, Dolgoff had little time for those who, seeking comfort or moral privilege in anarchist "purity," refuse to engage in the real struggles in which people find themselves. Anarchy cannot be abstracted from day-to-day life situations and the difficult choices with which people are confronted:

There is no "pure" anarchism. There is only the appli-cation of anarchist principles to the realities of social living. The aim of anarchism is to stimulate forces that propel society in a libertarian direction. It is only from this standpoint that the relevance of anarchism to modern life can be properly assessed. (1980, 8)

As Dolgoff concludes, anarchism is simply a "guide to action based on a realistic conception of social recon-struction" (1980, 10–11). Anarchists argue that for most of human history people have organized themselves collectively to satisfy their own needs. Social organization is conceived as a network of local voluntary groupings. Anarchists propose a decentralized society, without a central political body, in which people manage their own affairs free from any coercion or external authority. These self-governed communes could federate freely at regional (or larger) levels to ensure co-ordination or mutual defense. Their autonomy and specificity must be maintained, however. Each locality will decide freely which social, cultural and economic arrangements to pursue. Rather than a pyramid, anarchist associations would form a web. As Ward suggests: "Coordination requires neither uniformity nor bureaucracy" (2004, 89). Anarchists sometimes point to post offices and railway networks as examples of the way in which local groups and associations can combine to provide complex networks of functions without any central authority (Ward 2004). Postal services work as a result of voluntary agreements between different post offices, in different countries, without any central world postal authority (Ward 2004).

Anarchist organizing is built on what Ward calls "social and collective ventures rapidly growing into deeply rooted organizations for welfare and conviviality" (2004, 63). Unfortunately many of the relationships, practices, and resources that have allowed for the sustenance of human communities (and non-elites within class societies)—namely commons in land and labor—have been extinguished, marginalized, enclosed, or privatized within capitalist social systems. This has been an outcome of the ongoing conflict between commodification and the extension of commodity relations, and defense of the commons. It reflects the incursions of commodity forms throughout human and ecological communities and the displacement of common forms. Historically, this process is initiated through acts of violence and force (backed by legislation), regimes of what Marx terms primitive accumulation. Primitive accumulation expresses the assault of capital against the common social forms emphasized by Kropotkin, Landauer, and Dolgoff.

3.1: PRIMITIVE ACCUMULATION
CAPITAL AGAINST MUTUAL AID

Capitalist society consists largely of "the accumulation of life as work," to use Cleaver's apt description (1992a, 116). Valorization speaks to the processes by which capital can manage to put people to work, and to do so in such a way that the process is repeated on an ever-increasing scale. The structure of the wage, the division of labor and surplus value are all mechanisms through which exploitation is organized. Notably, the circuit of valorization involves circulation (exchange) as well as production.

Valorization expresses the fact that, from the perspective of capital, the specific character of each productive activity is unimportant, so long as that activity produces something that can, through its sale, realize enough surplus to allow the process to start all over again (Cleaver 1992a). The enormously diverse range of human activities, mental or physical, that people are capable of are rendered the same in the eyes of capital. What is important is that they can be put in the service of (exchange) value creation (for capital). More recently, autonomist theorists, including Antonio Negri and Michael Hardt, have discussed the ways in which contemporary capital makes use of "immaterial labor," especially emotional or psychological capacities that allow people to care for each other—a point that echoes historic anarchist concerns.

If valorization represents the subordination of people's productive activities to capitalist command, Cleaver (1992a, 120) suggests that disvalorization expresses people's loss of those abilities taken up by capital. This effects a broader impoverishment of social life as the specific qualities of a diversity of skills and abilities are replaced by a narrower range of commercialized, mechanized skills (Cleaver, 1992a).

A central and ongoing process in the history of capitalism is "the replacement of the self-production of use-values by the consumption of commodities" (Cleaver 1992a, 119). This is, in large part, what a whole series of practices—from the enclosures through colonialism more broadly—have been geared towards. This separation of people from the capacities for self-production of use-values has entailed the various forms of violence that Marx has called primitive accumulation. An ongoing process, primitive accumulation involves the actual, often bloody, practices by which capitalism takes over and commercializes growing areas of human life. This has included the clearing of peasants from common lands, the destruction of artisanal workshops, the canceling of local rights to the land, and the destruction of entire homes and villages. As Cleaver notes, a central aspect of primitive accumulation has been "the displacement of domestic food and handicraft production by capitalist commodities" (1992a, 119). Nowhere has the creation of the "home market" been established without such displacements:

> But of this we gain little insight from Marx. In his city-boy ignorance of rural life and perhaps in a desire to avoid any backward-looking sentimentalism, Marx seems to have spent little time or energy during his studies of primitive accumulation in England and in the colonies trying to understand what positive values might have been lost. Unlike many of his generation who did worry about the nature of those social ties and communal values which were rapidly disappearing, Marx kept his attention fixed firmly toward the future. (Cleaver 1992a, 122)

Interestingly, the response to primitive accumulation and its effects has historically been one of the key points distinguishing Marxists from anarchists. Anarchists have taken a vastly different, and less sanguine, approach to primitive accumulation from that taken by many Marxists, and certainly from the approach taken by Marx. Speaking about Marx, Cleaver notes:

> When we examine his writings on primitive accumulation and colonialism—from the *Communist Manifesto* to *Capital*—we often find little or no empathy for the cultures being destroyed/subsumed by capital. He certainly recognised such destruction/subsumption but frequently saw its effects on feudalism and other pre-capitalist forms of society as historically progressive.

> For Marx, workers were being liberated from pre-capitalist forms of exploitation (they 'escaped from the regime of the guilds') and peasants from 'serfdom' and 'the idiocy of rural life.' (1992a, 121)

Such an uncaring approach found its most widespread and influential expression within Marxism under the Second International view—that societies could not be revolutionary until they had entered the capitalist stage. This perspective was used among other things to argue against the possibility of revolution in Russia since it was a feudal rather than capitalist society.

Anarchists have been deeply concerned about exactly the values that have been lost. For anarchists, these lost abilities and skills extend beyond tasks of labor to include important elements of social life, such as decision-making or social interaction. Cleaver discusses this loss, and related issues of centralization and professionalization, in terms that are reminiscent of the historic anarchist analysis as discussed below:

> The rise of professional medicine, for example, not only produced a widespread loss of abilities to heal, but it also involved the substitution of one particular paradigm of healing for a much larger number of approaches to 'health', and thus an absolute social loss—the virtual disappearance of a multiplicity of alternative 'values.' (1992a, 120)

It is the attempt to identify, to understand, and to recover the values that have been lost, overlooked, or subsumed under capitalism that has inspired major anarchist projects whether Kropotkin's *Mutual Aid*, the works of Elisee Reclus or, more recently, David Graeber's *False Coin*.

More than the destruction of villages, workshops, farms or houses, primitive accumulation entails the destruction of entire ways of life, communities, and cultures. Primitive accumulation fundamentally involves the theft of people's independent means of production and living. Cleaver suggests that the very history of capitalism has been, fundamentally, "a history of a war on autonomous subsistence activities (what we might at this point call the history of disvalorisation)" (1992a, 124). He suggests that there has been such a war "because such subsistence activities have both survived and been repeatedly created anew—more so in some places than in others" (Cleaver 1992a, 124). It is in no way simply coincidental that primitive accumulation has been directed specifically at indigenous practices of gift economies, for example.

Related to these processes is the degrading of skills experienced by many workers and the monopolization of skilled labor by higher paid "mental workers" such as engineers. Opposing, and to some extent reversing, this replacement is a crucial, perhaps key, aspect of anarchist activity today. It is this opposition that underlies anarchist criticisms of the monopolization of learning skills by professional instructors or the monopolization of care-giving skills by professional social workers.

At the same time, anarchists are careful not to overestimate the success of capital's destructive power or to fail to appreciate the tenacity and perseverance of non-capitalist social relations. Indeed, a vast array of struggles against capitalism, both historically and contemporarily, has been based in precisely these supposedly "archaic" relations. As stated above, commonist forms of sociation and organization express the tenacity of archaic forms within capitalist societies. They express the persistence of the repressed sociological types exemplary of "mechanical solidarity" and *Gemeinschaft* within *Gesellschaft* social structures.

Commonists work to organize against dependency on commodities and professional "experts," the manifestations of the commodification of needs and market-supplied services. Commonists emphasize the significance of autonomous creativity in the struggles against states and capital.

They view these activities in terms of the possibilities for a post-capitalist future.

3.2: LINEAGES OF COMMONISM
KROPOTKIN AND MUTUAL AID

Among the primary historical influences on commonism, perhaps the most significant is Kropotkin's version of anarcho-communism and, especially, his ideas about mutual aid. In *Mutual Aid* Kropotkin documents the centrality of co-operation within animal and human groups and links anarchist theory with everyday experience. Kropotkin's definition suggests that anarchism, in part, "would represent an interwoven network, composed of an infinite variety of groups and federations of all sizes and degrees . . . temporary or more or less permanent . . . for all possible purposes" (quoted in Ward and Goodway 2003, 94). As Ward reminds us: "A century ago Kropotkin noted the endless variety of 'friendly societies, the unities of odd-fellows, the village and town clubs organised for meeting the doctors' bills' built up by working-class self-help" (2004, 29). Both Kropotkin and, to a much lesser extent, Marx, commented on and were inspired by peasant collaboration in various aspects of daily life, from the care of communal lands and forests, harvesting, the building of roads, house construction, and dairy production.

Kropotkin's political archeology, and especially his studies of the French Revolution and the Paris Commune, informed his analyses of the Russian revolutions of 1905 to 1917 and colored his warnings to comrades about the possibilities and perils that waited along the different paths of political change (Cleaver 1992b). This remains an important social and political undertaking in the context of crisis and structural adjustment impelled by the forces of capitalist globalization.

In 1917 Kropotkin saw the dangers in the crisis: both

> those of reaction and those disguised in the garb of
> revolution, whether parliamentary or Bolshevik . . . . In
> 1917 Kropotkin also knew where to look for the power
> to oppose those dangers and to create the space for the
> Russian people to craft their own solutions: in the self-
> activity of workers and peasants . . . . In 1917, as we
> know, the power of workers to resist both reaction and
> centralization proved inadequate—partly because the
> spokespersons of the later cloaked their intentions
> behind a bright rhetoric of revolution. Today . . . such
> rhetoric is no longer possible and in its place there is
> only the drab, alienating language of national and
> supranational state officials. (Cleaver 1992b, 10)

Kropotkin's vast research into mutual aid was motivated by
a desire to develop a general understanding of the character
of human societies and their processes of evolution. It was
partly concerned with providing a sociological critique of
the popular views of social Darwinists like Huxley and
Spencer. More than that, as Cleaver (1992b) notes, his work
was aimed at laying the foundation for his anarcho-
communist politics by showing a recurring tendency in
human societies, as well as in many other animal societies,
for individuals to help each other and to cooperate with
other members of the species rather than to compete in a
Hobbesian war of all against all.

In several book-length research works, including *Mutual Aid*, *The Conquest of Bread* and *Fields, Factories and
Workshops*, Kropotkin tried to sketch the manifestation and
development of mutual aid historically. What his research
suggested to him was that mutual aid was always present in
human societies, even if its development was never uniform
or the same over different periods or within different societies. At various points, mutual aid was the primary factor
of social life, while at other times it was submerged beneath
forces of competition, conflict, and violence. The key, however, was that regardless of its form or the adversity of cir-

cumstances in which it operated, it was always present, "providing the foundation for recurrent efforts at co-operative self-emancipation from various forms of domination (the state, institutional religion, capitalism)" (Cleaver 1992b, 3). Kropotkin was not, in a utopian manner, trying to suggest how a new society might or should develop. In his view, it was already happening. The instances were already appearing in the present.

This highlights a crucial feature of commonist approaches. Commonism is not about the drawing up of social blueprints for the future. Similarly anarchists, to this day, have been quite reluctant to describe the "anarchist society." Instead, anarchists have tried mainly to identify and understand social trends or tendencies, even countervailing ones, by which social relations can be sustained over time outside of states and capital. The focus is resolutely on manifestations of the future, post-statist, post-capitalist community, in the present.

In major works such as *The Conquest of Bread*, Kropotkin sought to detail how the post-capitalist future was already emerging in the here and now of everyday life. His research in this case was concerned with, and indeed managed to offer examples of, practical cases in the present; this suggested aspects of a post-capitalist community. In this way, Kropotkin's work (as with the work of other anarcho-communists) offers something more than simply a proposition. Thus, his politics were grounded in ongoing, if under-appreciated, aspects of human societies (Cleaver 1992b).

Kropotkin argued that human societies developed through processes involved in the ongoing interplay of what he called the "law of mutual struggle" and the "law of mutual aid." These forces manifested themselves in various ways depending on historical period or social context, but significantly for Kropotkin, they were typically observed in conflict or interaction rather than in stasis or equilibrium. Neither was this strictly an evolutionary schema, since

Kroptkin includes periods of revolutionary upheaval within his view of the interplay between these forces.

> On the one side were the institutions and behaviors of mutual struggle such as narrow-minded individualism, competition, the concentration of landed and industrial property, capitalist exploitation, the state and war. On the other side were those of mutual aid such as cooperation in production, village folkmotes, communal celebrations, trade unionism and syndicalism, strikes, political and social associations. (Cleaver 1992b, 4)

According to Kropotkin, one or the other force tended to be predominant depending on the era or circumstances, but it was his considered opinion that forces of mutual aid were on the rise, even as capitalism appeared triumphant. In fact, in his view, the sort of industrial development for which capitalism was famous could not be possible without an incredible degree of co-operative labor. Kropotkin argued against capitalist myth-making that presented the rapid growth of industrial development as the result of competition and instead suggested that the scope and efficiency of cooperation were more important factors (see Cleaver 1992b). In this, his analysis was remarkably close to that of Marx, who indeed saw the mass co-operation of industrial production as a prerequisite for communism.

> Where economists emphasized static comparative advantage, Kropotkin demonstrated the dynamic countertendency toward increasing complexity and interdependence (cooperation) among industries—a development closely associated with the unstoppable international circulation of knowledge and experience. Where the economists (and later the sociologists of work) celebrated the efficacy and productivity of specialization in production, Kropotkin showed how

that very productivity was based not on competition but on the interlinked efforts of only formally divided workers. (Cleaver 1992b, 5)

Commonists might do well to remember Kropotkin's advice concerning the methods to be followed by anarchist researchers. In his 1887 book, *Anarchist Communism*, Kropotkin suggests that the anarchist approach differs from that of the utopian: "[The anarchist] studies human society as it is now and was in the past . . . tries to discover its tendencies, past and present, its growing needs, intellectual and economic, and in his [sic] ideal he [sic] merely points out in which direction evolution goes" (quoted in Cleaver 1992b, 3).

This focus on tendencies, or developing patterns of concrete behavior, differentiated his approach from both early utopians and later Marxist-Leninists by abandoning the Kantian "ought" in favor of the scientific study of what is already coming to be. Neither Fourier nor Owen hesitated to spell out the way they felt society ought to be organized, from cooperatives to *phalansteries*. Nor were Lenin and his Bolshevik allies reluctant to specify, in considerable detail, the way work should be organized (Taylorism and competition) and how social decision-making ought to be arranged (top down through party administration and central planning. (Cleaver 1992b, 3)

Marx's writings offered much less detail than Kropotkin's works when it comes to the issue of working class subjecttivity, in contrast to the rather extensive analysis Marx provided with regard to capitalist domination. It was only through the decades of work carried out by various autonomist Marxists that there was developed any Marxist analysis of working class autonomy that came close to a parallel of Kropotkin's work (Cleaver 1992b, 7).

The collapse of the "actually existing" socialist states and the crisis-inducing development of capitalist globalization have in various ways impelled a re-thinking of issues of social transformation and the surpassing of capitalism by anarchists as well as Marxists. Various streams of anarcho-communism, most notably those that are part of the stream of everyday anarchy, from Kropotkin to Goodman to Ward, can be seen to have strong similarities, or even affinities, with certain traditions of libertarian or autonomist Marxism. This is especially so when one considers the anarcho-communist and libertarian Marxist approaches to the questions of constructing alternatives to capitalism in the here and now. There are striking similarities, for example, between autonomist Marxist writings on self-valorization and anarchist writings on mutual aid and affinity. The types of concrete actually existing mutual aid activities initiated or supported by anarchists certainly embody the notion of self-valorization and the self-constitution of alternative modes of living, as discussed by Cleaver (1992a). These are autonomous self-valorizing activities that, as discussed again by autonomists, are confronted by capitalist attempts at disvalorization.

As noted above, Harry Cleaver (1992b) finds a great resonance, especially, between the analyses of Peter Kropotkin (and his concern with the emergence of a new society from within capitalism) and the analyses of autonomist Marxists who suggest that the future might be glimpsed within current processes of working-class self-valorization, or those autonomous practices by which people attempt to create alternative social relations, either at work or in their communities. Cleaver notes that, as "a replacement for an exhausted and failed orthodoxy," the autonomist Marxists offer a more vital and engaged Marxism, "one that has been regenerated within the struggles of real people and as such, has been able to articulate at least some elements of their desires and projects of self-valorization" (1992b, 11). Given this close political affinity, Cleaver suggests that, against more sectarian positions, those inspired by Kropotkin might do well to pay attention to the libertarian Marxists just as the Marxists might find inspiration for their own work in Kropotkin's efforts (1992b). I would agree and suggest that contemporary anarchists, who have tended to eschew analyses of class, can gain much especially through an engagement with autonomist Marxist ideas of self-valorization. Self-valorization helps to create some broader possibilities for people, individually and collectively, to take further actions to act in their own interests and to gain greater opportunities for the self-determination of larger parts of their lives.

Anarchists try to avoid a productivist vision of life, emphasizing the great diversity of ways in which human life might be realized. Anarchists again share common ground with autonomist Marxists in arguing that the only way that work can be an interesting mode of self-realization for people is "through its subordination to the rest of life, the exact opposite of capitalism" (Cleaver 1992a, 143, n. 59). Commonists of various stripes are attempting to organize their productive activities, and to extend this organization, in order to initially impede and to eventually break capitalist command over society.

What is common in the approach taken by Kropotkin to the issue of superceding capitalism and that taken by the autonomist Marxists is the emphasis on manifestations of the future in the present. The shared concern is with, as Cleaver suggests, "the identification of already existing activities which embody new, alternative forms of social cooperation and ways of being" (1992b, 10). Autonomist Marxists, like anarchists, emphasize the primary importance of the self-activity and creativity of people in struggle.

The attempt to reconceptualize the process of moving beyond capitalism, as developed in the works of autonomist

Marxists, bears quite striking similarities to the approach offered by Kropotkin regarding this question (Cleaver 1992b). Autonomist Marxists share with most anarchists a rejection of concepts of "the transitional period" or "the transitional program." In place of "the transition," autonomists and anarchists emphasize some version of what Hakim Bey calls "immediatism," or activities that suggest the revolution is already underway.

The focus on workers' autonomy has led to a rejection of orthodox Marxist arguments that the transcendence of capitalism and movement to a post-capitalist society requires some form of transitional order (i.e. socialism) characterized by party management of the state in the name of the people (Cleaver 1992b). Autonomist Marxists' emphasis on the autonomy of working class self-activity stresses not only autonomy from capital but also autonomy from the "official" organizations of the working class, especially from trade unions and socialist (or more specifically, social democratic) parties. This approach shares with anarchism an analysis of the Russian revolution of 1917 that saw the Bolshevik takeover of the soviets as the beginning of the restoration of domination and exploitation (Cleaver 1992b). Thus the subversion of the revolution is viewed as occurring much earlier than with the emergence of Stalinism, to which most Leninists and Trotskyists point as the moment that marked the revolution's betrayal.

Autonomists, like anarchists, argue that the process of building a new society must be the work of the people themselves, lest it be doomed from the outset. Class struggle has a dual character, and its categories can be understood from either the perspective of capital or the perspective of the working class. The shift in focus away from capital—the domain of orthodox Marxist approaches—towards workers has opened new realizations, including a recognition that the "working class" is itself a category of capital, and, crucially, one that people have struggled to avoid or escape (Cleaver 1992b, 7).

3.4: CONCLUSION

Unlike utopian thinkers, commonists tend to avoid discussing "blueprints" of future social relations, or at least exercise extreme caution when they do so. Commonists contend that it is always up to those seeking freedom to decide how they desire to live. Still, there are a few features characteristic of commonist visions of a free society. While not in agreement about the means to bring about the future libertarian society, commonists are clear that means and ends cannot be separated.

> The moment we stop insisting on viewing all forms of action only by their function in reproducing larger, total, forms of inequality of power, we will also be able to see that anarchist social relations and non-alienated forms of action are all around us. And this is critical because it already shows that anarchism is, already, and has always been, one of the main bases for human interaction. We self-organize and engage in mutual aid all the time. We always have. (Graeber 2004, 76)

Commonist communities must, almost by definition, be based upon ongoing experiments in social arrangements, in confronting the ongoing dilemma of maintaining both individual freedoms and social equality (Ehrlich 1996). The revolution is always in the making. These projects make up what the anarchist sociologist Howard Ehrlich calls "anarchist transfer cultures."

> Despite the dominant authoritarian trend in existing society, most contemporary anarchists therefore try and extend spheres of free action in the hope that they will one day become the mainstream of social life. In difficult times, they are, like Paul Goodman, revolutionary conservatives, maintaining older traditions of mutual aid and free enquiry when under threat. In

more auspicious moments, they move out from free
zones until by their example and wisdom they begin to
convert the majority of people to their libertarian
vision. (Marshall 1992, 659)

Constructive anarchists recognize that revolutions do not
emerge fully formed from nothing. There is a pressing need,
in pre-revolutionary times, for institutions, organizations,
and relations that can sustain people as well as building
capacities for self-defense and struggle. These I have termed
infrastructures of resistance (Shantz 2008).

04: Commonism and Post-Political Politics
Gifts, Self-Valorization, and the Coming Communities

As an alternative to the market valorization and production for profit embodied in capitalist enterprises, commonists turn to self-valorizing production rooted in the needs, experiences, and desires of specific communities. In place of a consumerist ethos that encourages consumption of ready-made items, commonists adopt a productivist ethos that attempts a re-integration of production and consumption. At the same time, their practice articulates what might be termed a post-political politics. This politics is post-political in the sense that it rejects notions of politics based on representation, in general, particularly representation at the level of the state.

In attempting to re-think social activity in the current context I focus on overlooked or under-appreciated themes, priorities, and forms of creativity that pose important challenges to conventional thinking about politics. The key principles of contemporary practices that I identify and examine in the following sections of this work are self-valorization, or creative work outside and against capitalist valorization for the market, do-it-yourself (DIY) politics, and collaborative "ownership" and the gift economy. Taken together, these aspects of movement practice express a striving for autonomy and self-determination rather than a politics of representation.

4.1: COMMONIST EXCHANGE
THE GIFT

There have been numerous anarchist projects based on notions of the gift economy. Projects like TAO Communications, Food Not Bombs, and the Anarchist Free School are all based largely on economies of gift presentation (not necessarily based on exchange). Also, anarchists have played important parts in developing aspects of the gift economy in broader projects such as the Internet and open source software such as Linux.

Among the most influential writings on gift economies are those of Marcel Mauss, a "founder" of French anthropology. In addition to his anthropological research, Mauss was a revolutionary socialist who was active in the consumer cooperative movement in France. Mauss argued that socialism would never come "from above" through any type of state apparatus, regardless of the self-proclaimed character of that state. Mauss followed the anarchists of his day in suggesting that the beginnings of a new socialist society could be constructed in the shell of the old capitalist one through practices of mutual aid and self-organization. In practical terms, Mauss saw the development of an anti-capitalist economy coming from efforts to build and coordinate grassroots cooperative projects. According to Graeber, Mauss "felt that existing popular practices provided the basis both for a moral critique of capitalism and possible glimpses of what a future society would be like" (2004, 18). Mauss was deeply troubled by the direction socialism was being taken in the Soviet Union under Lenin, especially the reintroduction of the market under the New Economic Program (NEP) in the 1920s. Graeber sums up Mauss's overriding concern for socialist development:

If it was impossible to simply legislate the money economy away, even in Russia, the least monetarized society in Europe, then perhaps revolutionaries needed to start looking at the ethnographic record to see what sort of creature the market really was, and what viable alternatives to capitalism might look like. (2004, 17)

In his "Essay on the Gift" (1925), Mauss argued that the basis of contracts and exchange was not, as economists have tended to claim, in barter. His studies suggested that there has never been an economy based on barter. Instead, the origins of contracts and exchange in non-monetary economies rests in communism or "an unconditional commitment to another's needs" (Graeber 2004, 17). Rather than barter, the key economic practice of non-monetary societies has been the exchange of gifts. Within these gift economies "the distinctions we now make between interest and altruism, person and property, freedom and obligation, simply did not exist" (Graeber 2004, 17).

Mauss rejected popular views that stateless or market-less societies were simply underdeveloped "pre-state" or "pre-market" societies in a teleological schema that had yet to unfold properly. Prior to Mauss's work, the assumption in much of the West had been that marketless economies were trying to participate in market behavior, but simply "hadn't yet developed very sophisticated ways of going about it" (Graeber 2004, 21). Instead, Mauss (1925) suggested that stateless and marketless societies were structured the way they were because that was the manner in which their members wanted to live. Even more, rather than foreshadowing the market in their economic interactions, notably through barter activities, those societies actually operated according to a logic that is in many ways antithetical to the market. Rather than economies of barter, these were economies of the gift.

In his compelling and provocative essay, "The High-

Tech Gift Economy" (1998), Richard Barbrook argues that the gift economy provides a starting point for thinking about social relations beyond either the state or market. More than that, the gift economy provides the basis for an incipient anarcho-communism, visions of which have inspired a variety of recent community media and "do-it-yourself" (DIY) cultural activism. Despite the contributions Barbrook's article makes to a rethinking of both emergent social movements and alternatives to statist capitalism, his emphasis on gift exchange leaves his analysis at the level of consumption and exchange, rather than addressing crucial issues of production. Yet it is predominantly questions of production, and especially the transformation of production relations, that has motivated anarcho-communists historically. I want to look more closely, if briefly, at the contestatory and transformative aspects hinted at by DIY production within the gift economy. Such production, more than issues of how exchange occurs, suggest possibilities for eluding or challenging relations of capitalist value production. Crucial for understanding the liberatory potential of the "new economy" beyond the practices of consumption or exchange, is the notion of self-valorization or production which emphasizes community (use) values rather than capitalist value.

4.2: COMMONIST PRODUCTION
SELF-VALORIZATION

The notion of self-valorization, as used by contemporary anarchists and libertarian communists, builds upon Marx's discussion of use value versus exchange value. People produce things because they have some kind of use for them; they meet some need or desire. This is where the qualitative aspect of production comes in. Generally, people prefer products that are well-made, function as planned, are not poisonous and so on. Under capitalism, exchange value, (in which a coat can get two pairs of shoes) predominates over use value. This is the quantitative aspect of value that doesn't indicate whether the product is durable, shoddy or toxic as long as it secures its (potential) value in sale or other exchange with something else.

And capitalism's driving focus on the quantitative at the expense of the qualitative also comes to dominate human labor. The quality (skill, pleasure, creativity) of the particular work that people do isn't primarily relevant for the capitalist (except that skilled labour costs more to produce and carries more exchange value). That's partly because exchange is based on the quantity of 'average-socially-necessary-labour-time' embodied in the product human labor produces. That simply means that if some firm takes a longer time to produce something on outdated machinery they can't claim the extra labor time they take, due to inefficiencies, compared to a firm that produces more quickly using updated technology, and that's one reason why outmoded producers go under).

Capitalist production is geared towards exchange as the only way that surplus value is actually realized rather than being potential; the capitalist can't bank surplus as value until the product has been exchanged. Use value plays a part only to the extent that something has to have some use for people or else they would not buy it; well, if the thing seems totally useless the bosses still have advertising to convince people otherwise. Under other non-capitalist "modes of production," such as feudalism, most production is geared towards use value production rather than exchange value. For Marx, under communist social relations there is no exchange value, what is produced will still retain use value.

Surely if, under communism, people are producing to meet their needs, they will continue to produce use values (and even a surplus of them in case of emergency) without regard for exchange value (which would, certainly, be absent in a truly communist society anyway). Unless one is talking about a communism of uselessness perhaps. Certainly people would value their work (qualitatively) in ways that cannot be imagined now since they would be meeting their community's needs and would try to do so with some joy and pleasure in work, providing decent products without fouling up the environment.

As Barbrook (1998) suggests, for participants in a diversity of contemporary affinity groups, DIY activities offer a context for coming together, a shared opportunity for mutual expression and unalienated labor. Contemporary usage of the term DIY in underground movements comes from punk rock and its visceral attack on the professionalization of rock, as well as the related distance between fans and rock stars. This anti-hierarchical perspective and the practices that flow from it are inspired by a deep longing for self-determined activity that eschews reliance on the products of corporate culture.

It is perhaps highly telling that, in an age of multinational media conglomerates and gargantuan publishing monopolies, a number of younger people have turned towards artisanal forms of craft production in order to produce and distribute what are often very personal works. Even more than this, however, are the means of production, involving collective decision-making as well as collective labor in which participants are involved, to the degree that they wish to be, in all aspects of the process from conception through to distribution.

While cultural theorist Walter Benjamin spoke of disenchantment in the "age of mechanical reproduction" (1969), DIY projects offer expressions of re-enchantment or authenticity. This authenticity is grounded at least in the sense that such works help to overcome the division between head and hand that reflects the division of labor in a society of mass-produced representation. As attempts to overcome alienation and address concerns with overly mediated activities, DIY activities suggest a striving for what an earlier era might have called control over the means of production, and what has now come to include control over the means of representation. Perhaps iron-ically, this has been aided by the availability of inexpensive desktop publishing and other means of "mechanical repro-duction" since the 1980s (though not all anarchists choose to use it).

Impulses behind the turn to self-production include a desire for cultural autonomy along with a preference for decentralized, local, and participatory forms of commu-nication, and concerns over questions of representation. Along with DIY production often comes the collective production of alternative subjectivities. More often than not, the commonist producers carry out their work in collectively run community centers, or infoshops—the modern version of the craft cottage right in the heart of the inner city. A visit to an infoshop, such as Wooden Shoe books in Philadelphia or Spartacus in Vancouver, will generally reveal a variety of original self-made works.

For many, the content as well as the process of commonist production expresses a confrontation with the cultural codes of everyday life. While such activities express a variety of styles and viewpoints, they tend to present a vision of a desired society that is participatory and demo-cratic. In production, content, and often through distri-bution in gift economies, they advocate active production of culture rather than passive consumption of cultural (or even entertainment) commodities. Self-production pro-vides an opportunity for producers to act against the pro-prietorship of information. Most commonist communica-tions (whether literature, music, videos, or broadcasts) are produced as anti-copyrights, or as "copy-lefts," where the sharing of material is encouraged. Indeed, as a key part of gift economies, DIY takes on an important place in experimenting with communities that are not organized around market principles of exchange value. They help to create a culture of self-valorization rather than giving creativity over to the logics of surplus value.

4.3: COLLABORATIVE PRODUCTION AND THE
COMMONIST ECONOMY

Commonist DIY production raises the key contemporary question—one that is socially and politically charged—of whether collaborative production and ownership in diverse areas, and the growth of opportunities for collaboration enabled partly through new technologies, might pose a serious challenge to the hegemony of international property rights regimes. Collaborative ownership historically extends throughout human communities and finds vibrant contemporary expressions in a variety of places, including academic research, open source software, and community service networks. At the same time, collaborative ownership is more than ever before being confronted by powerful institutions and organizations, with the full weight of multinational corporations and national states behind them, seeking to extend the private control and management of both the processes and products of creative activities.

As Rishab Ghosh (2005a) suggests, intellectual property rights and policy decisions that treat knowledge and art as physical forms of property, far from enhancing creativity, actually limit public access to creativity and discourage collaborative creative efforts while threatening to decrease creativity overall. For Ghosh, a clear indicator of the extent of the conversion from knowledge and art to "intellectual property" is the widespread assumption that creative production is necessarily individual and private, with collaboration occurring only under commercial conditions. Collaboration, as in open source software development where thousands of people might organize informally without ever meeting to produce high quality works, is often viewed as being an exception. Even more, this exceptionality is often explained as having a predominantly ideological basis. As Ghosh suggests, there is a somewhat romanticized notion that collaborative production and ownership on a large scale are driven by ideology and require the commitment of idealists in order to occur (2005b, 1).

Lost in hegemonic neoliberal discourses of proprietary rights and market competitiveness is the recognition of human sociality—that the greatest human achievements have been collaborative efforts. In the current context, as Ghosh notes, collaboratively creating knowledge has come to be viewed as a novelty (2005a, 3). As Ghosh suggests: "Newton should have had to pay a license fee before being allowed even to see how tall the 'shoulders of giants' were, let alone to stand upon them" (2005a, 3). At the same time, DIY movements have played important parts in renewing public interest in collaborative creation more broadly.

Yet a strong and compelling case can be made that collaborative approaches to creativity are desirable and viable alternatives to proprietary frameworks based on widespread and strongly enforced intellectual property regimes. A great strength of the recent anarchist approaches is the interest in exploring creativity from a diversity of perspectives, including not only economics, law, and software development, but also anthropology. Examples of recent and historic collaborative approaches range over collective ownership in indigenous societies, academic science, and free software to name only a few cases that bring a historical perspective to bear on real world experiences. This leads to the examining of creativity and the collaborative ownership of knowledge in different times and places to illustrate that collaboration is far from being a novel aspect of human societies.

Many analyses of collaborative and non-monetary production in new economies, such as free software or the Internet, use the descriptor of gift-giving that supposedly characterizes "tribal" societies. Exchange within such societies is posed as consisting of the altruistic offering of gifts without expectations of exchanges. This description is popular in discussions of a variety of contemporary practices, and is used to explain activities ranging from informal economies to do-it-yourself subcultures.

Some anthropologists, however, suggest that production and exchange within tribal societies are more complexly arranged than is suggested by notions of altruistic gift-giving. Various anthropological accounts suggest that tribal societies engage in non-monetary or non-proprietary forms of production and exchange in a manner that builds complex webs of reciprocal obligation that bind members together (Ghosh 2005b, 7). The evidence presented in these anthropological works suggests that gift giving in tribal societies is carried out within a context of reciprocity and expected returns, either in terms of status, rights, or more gifts.

At the same time, the anthropological accounts suggest that there are relevant similarities between collaborative production, non-monetary exchange in tribal societies, and collaborative ownership in the digital economy (Ghosh 2005b, 7). In refining altruistic notions of the gift economy, however, these anthropologists argue that, in many cases, gift-giving is based on the self-interested participation of individuals and communities connected through complex webs of rights and obligations.

This is not to be taken, as property rights advocates might wish, as an argument against notions of the gift economy, but rather is offered to suggest the multiple and complex manifestations of collaborative production and non-monetary exchange with human communities. Strathern, for example, shows that in certain communities of Papua New Guinea, one sees, rather than true collective ownership, multiple ownership or multiple authorship, where each "owner" might claim a definable but inseparable part of a collectively owned whole (2005). Similarly, Leach explores multiple ownership through a comparison of local practices in the Madang area of Papua New Guinea and global contributions to Linux development (2005). In both cases, individual contributions, even where they can be clearly identified, have no value outside of the collaboratively produced whole of which they are part. Leach makes the crucial point that the nature of ownership is based substantially on the mode of production and the processes of creation (2005). This point is reinforced in the works of several anarchist anthropologists, such as Pierre Clastres, David Graeber, or Harold Barclay, whose works explore, on the basis of extensive anthropological evidence, collaborative production and distribution that is not motivated by concerns with exchange. For such alternative perspectives the reader might wish to consult Barclay's *People Without Government* (1990) or, more recently, Graeber's *Toward an Anthropological Theory of Value* (2001).

At the same time, Ghosh makes explicit his preference for analysis based on rational actors concerned with "balancing their *value-flows*" (2005c, 111). For Ghosh, the self-interested people engaged in collaborative production will do so as long as they take more from it than they put in. While most collaborative work occurs without clearly identified one-to-one transactions, as Ghosh recognizes, the author still insists on modeling collaborative participants as making rational self-interested contributions as long as benefits are greater than costs.

One should always be cautious about attempts to use rather conventional economic analysis to explain complex social relations and practices, and Ghosh's reliance on such limited theories is quite unsatisfactory. Given the rather extensive sociological literature contesting the claims of rational choice theories, the absence of a sociological analysis is a glaring omission here.

More nuanced and convincing arguments are offered by Yochai Benkler (2005). Moving beyond rational choice perspectives, Benkler provides an interesting discussion of systems of collaborative production that are sustained without direct reference to the benefits accruing to individual participants (2005). Benkler notes that the Internet has enabled structures of production that are sustained even where the motives of contributors do not appear to be driven by a "rational choice" for individual rewards (2005).

Some anarchists and libertarian Marxists have pursued the notion that the growing application of property rights to knowledge and creativity is in fact a new enclosure movement, similar to the enclosures of common land during the period of capitalism's emergence from feudalism. Indeed it might be suggested that an increasingly vigorous application of the language of property rights to knowledge and creativity represents an enclosure of the mind.

If the imposition of property regimes on knowledge and creativity constitutes a second enclosure movement, then what, one might ask, is emerging as the equivalent of the Diggers or Ranters? Against more pessimistic accounts of the new enclosures, John Clippinger and David Bollier suggest that the growing global acclaim for free software heralds the beginnings of a renaissance of the commons (2005). The anarchists and punks who undertake DIY productive activities provide one example of what the new Diggers might look like. At the same time, current (and proposed) international trade policies pose tangible threats to the future of the knowledge commons and collaboration.

4.4: COMMONIST COUNTER-POWER?

The arguments made concerning gift economies find an interesting parallel in the political realm within the more recent research of the French anthropologist Pierre Clastres, whose works, it might be noted, influenced the writings of Deleuze and Guattari. Clastres wrote against the teleogical perspective within much political anthropology, which saw the state as a more efficient form of organization, an advancement that superseded the forms that had preceded it (see Graeber 2004).

Clastres' primary research involved stateless Amazonian societies that were assumed within mainstream political anthropology not to have achieved the same level of development as the Aztecs or the Inca. Clastres, however, did not accept this conceptualization, which he saw as reflecting the biases of Western political economy:

> But what if, he proposed, Amazonians were not en-
> tirely unaware of what the elementary forms of state
> power might be like—what it would mean to allow
> some men to give everyone else orders which could not
> be questioned, since they were backed up by the threat
> of force—and were for that very reason determined to
> ensure such things never came about? (Graeber, 2004,
> 22)

One of the most important insights offered by Clastres is that non-statist societies seem well aware of the dangers posed by concentrations of power, and spend much of their community life engaged in efforts to ward off such con-centrations. Such societies organize to ensure that no one gains control over economic resources that might be wielded in constraining the freedom of others, as well as to ensure that no one is subjected to the orders of another (Clastres, 1989, 1994; see also Bey 1991; 1996). Clastres (1989; 1994) suggests that this is one explanation for the periodic inner conflicts and symbolic violence that mark generally egalitarian societies. This goes beyond conven-tional political notions of counter-power in which dissident groups establish institutions, such as alternative comm-unities or radical co-operatives, by which the state and capital might be opposed. Clastres's work has further implications for anarchists:

> It suggests that counterpower, at least in the most
> elementary sense, actually exists where the states and
> markets are not even present; that in such cases, rather
> than being embodied in popular institutions which
> pose themselves against the power of lords, or kings, or
> plutocrats, they are embodied in institutions which

> ensure such types of person never come about. (Graeber 2004, 25)

This is a power that is counter not only to a present and operational power, but, beyond that, to a latent or potential power. Graeber (2004, 25) suggests that this is an opposition to the very "dialectical possibility" of concentrated power "within the society itself." The symbolic violence that marks many relatively egalitarian societies seems to arise from the many tensions involved in maintaining egalitarian social relations (Clastres 1989; 1994).

Peter Lamborn Wilson (Hakim Bey) returns the notion of "war machine" to its roots in Clastre's anthropology by using the term "Clastrian machine" to speak of the mechanisms that are deployed to ward off the emergence of concentrated power and domination (1996). Anarchists such as Bey suggest that, taken together, the work of Mauss and Clastres begins the groundwork for a theory of revolutionary counter-power. In this view, such an approach can provide an interesting perspective within which theories of value and theories of resistance might be synthesized:

> Institutionally, counterpower takes the form of what we would call institutions of direct democracy, consensus and mediation; that is, ways of publicly negotiating and controlling that inevitable internal tumult and transforming it into those social states (or if you like, forms of value) that society sees as the most desirable: conviviality, unanimity, fertility, prosperity, beauty, however it may be framed. (Graeber 2004, 35)

For contemporary anarchists, counter-power is rooted in the imaginative work of identification with others that makes understanding possible. Institutionally, it provides an impetus both for the creation of new social forms and/or the transformation or revalorization of old ones.

4.5: THEORETICAL AFFINITIES
COMMONISM AND THE COMING COMMUNITIES

In order to develop social theories that are attuned to recently developing social movement practices and perspectives, especially concerning issues of non-representationalism, a growing number of contemporary anarchists (most notably Hakim Bey, Todd May, Richard Day and Andrew Koch) have turned to the disparate works of Michel Foucault, Gilles Deleuze and Felix Guattari. The most extensive attempt to begin a re-thinking of social movements through an engagement with these authors has come from Richard Day and his attempt to articulate rather abstract postmodern writings on state forms with the practical political writings of anarchists.

Foucault offers an analytics of power and an ethic of care for the self which allows him to differentiate between various modalities of power relations. In this perspective one can give oneself rules that allow for power to be exercised with a minimum of domination (which minimizes relations of domination). Power is always present, but how is it practiced? What kinds of power?

Foucault makes a distinction between "liberties" and "states of domination," a distinction that is actually quite similar to distinctions made by anarchists Gustav Landauer and Rudolph Rocker. Liberties represent "live" relations of power in which most of the players, most of the time, have some ability to alter the situations in which they find themselves. Within states of domination, the flow (or process) of power has "congealed" or been blocked, preventing movement for some of the players most of the time. This represents a "dead" power brought about by specific "techniques of government."

At this point, a third type of power relation emerges: struggle or resistance. Local and regional practices of resistance are one way in which groups can work against relations of domination. Another way is by exerting "control over oneself" so one does not "give in to an urge to exercise tyrannical control over others" (Day 2001, 31).

Day (2001) is unsatisfied by these negative responses. Instead he asks about positive possibilities for social action and transformation. To do so he turns to Deleuze and Guattari for boldly constructive social criticism and the creation of alternatives, including new concepts of society and new concepts of social relations. Deleuze and Guattari utilize a network of contingent dualisms to enable their critique of particular power relations, and Day finds this particularly useful for thinking about contemporary politics.

At the level of structure, Deleuze and Guattari identify arborescent and rhizomatic forms of organization. Arborescent forms consisting of "hierarchical systems with centres of significance and subjectification,"operating through unidirectional "chains of command," are characteristic of contemporary Western societies. Conversely rhizomatic forms consist of "acentred systems, finite networks . . . in which communication runs from any neighbour to any other" (Day 2001, 33). Local operations are coordinated without a central agency. No one is in control, decisions are emergent, as are the identities and connections by which they are made.

Also important is the distinction made by Deleuze and Guattari between state forms and war-machines. State forms represent apparatuses of capture "that bring 'outside' elements 'inside' by connecting them up with an arborescent system" (Day 2001, 33). War machines are exterior to state apparatuses and work to undo the bonds of state capture. Notably, however, states operate in competition and co-operation with war-machines. States perpetuate arborescent forms while war-machines tend to destroy old forms and initiate new ones through rhizomatic connections.

States can, and indeed they must, incorporate war-machines, tame them, and put them to use in "an institutionalized army." They must be made part of the "general police" function, which includes practices of the social citizenship state, which have been a part of drawing subordinate classes under the state's police function as reflected in welfare policies and policies around homelessness among others.

In order to ward off development of the state form, social movements need to set up lateral affiliations and a system of networks and popular bases. This system would provide bases for social forces that neither ask for gifts from the state (as in the liberal-democratic new social movements) nor seek state power themselves (as in classical Marxism). In Day's words, they resist the will to domination in favor of affinity (2001).

For Richard Day, today we require an analysis of the relation of projects of social transformation with "actually existing democracy." Despite the contributions of the liberal-democratic state (redistribution of wealth, "rights" enforcement), liberal democracy "remains a frighteningly arborescent form which relies upon dead power to achieve its effects." The analysis undertaken by contemporary anarchists is, for Day, compatible with a move away from subject positions associated with the system of liberal-capitalist nation-states, in favor of identifications produced by what Giorgio Agamben has called "coming communities" (Agamben 1993). Such a perspective provides a way to think about "community without universality" and "history without teleology." For Agamben, the task of contemporary politics will no longer be "a struggle for conquest or control" of power as domination, but will involve the creation of "a community with neither presuppositions nor a State" (Agamben 1993, 82).

4.6: CONCLUSION

Recently, there have emerged a variety of experiments with alternative forms of social and economic organization, as part of broader struggles against capitalist globalization. These experiments provide alternatives to capitalist economic rationality, if only in embryonic form. Shorthose suggests that these "micro-experiments," such as those discussed above, present "the potential for a more convivial and sustainable future as well as empowering individuals to maintain a greater sense of economic security and an expanded sphere of autonomy away from the vagaries of the market" (2000, 191). These experiments go beyond the ephemeral manifestations of protest politics to begin the work of putting forward an alternative infrastructure, both for the day-to-day necessities of sustaining movements in struggle as well as to provide a space for developing social, economic, and political relationships that prefigure the sorts of relationships that people would like to see replace those that characterize those of contemporary capitalism.

The movements against capitalist production, the affinity-based relations they have developed, and their emphasis on self-valorizing activities suggest not only an opposition to global capital's economic rationality and its statist supports, but also suggest a yearning for economic, social, and political alternatives to that rationality. In addition, they articulate theoretical alternatives to the representation and interpretation that accompany it.

DIY production, including the production of media (immediately and relatively inexpensively produced), contribute to the creation of alternative spaces and relations from which to counter hostile or inaccurate mass media representations of the subculture. The commonist producers are not asking for improved representation in the manner of some producers of "alternative media," but are instead trying to tell their own stories. Commonist producers assert control over the means of re/presentation while challenging the very real material constraints on participation in the social and cultural environment.

Finally, it might be said that commonist production offers what an earlier generation of anarchists called "propaganda of the deed." In the physical work of collectively self-producing, working together, there is also a symbolic production—a production of alternative meanings about culture, work, and community.

For many contemporary activists and theorists, the concept of self-valorization offers an important starting point for thinking about "the circuits that constitute an alternative sociality, autonomous from the control of the State or capital" (Hardt 1996, 6). Originating in autonomist Marxist reflections on the social movements that emerged most notably in Italy during the intense struggles of the 1970s, recent notions of self-valorization has influenced a range of libertarian communist and anarchist writers. As Hardt suggests,

> Self-valorization was a principal concept that circulated in the movements, referring to social forms and structures of value that were relatively autonomous from and posed an effective alternative to capitalist circuits of valorization. Self-valorization was thought of as the building block for constructing a new form of sociality, a new society. (1996, 3)

Twentieth-century notions of self-valorization echo the arguments made by classical anarchist communists such as Kropotkin and Reclus, regarding the construction of grassroots forms of welfare developed through mutual aid societies. Self-valorization is one way by which a variety of recent theorists have sought to identify social forms of welfare that might constitute alternative networks outside of state control (Hardt 1996; see also Vercellone 1996 and Del Re 1996). As Del Re suggests, part of the new parameters for change includes "the proposal to go beyond welfare by taking as our goal the improvement of the quality of life, starting from the reorganization of the time of our lives" (1996, 110).

For radical political theorists, especially those engaged

with libertarian expressions of Italian Marxism, the experiences of the social movements

> show the possibilities of alternative forms of welfare in which systems of aid and socialization are separated from State control and situated instead in autonomous social networks. These alternative experiments may show how systems of social welfare will survive the crisis of the Welfare State. (Vercellone 1996, 81)

These systems of social welfare, however, are based on social solidarity (outside of state control) through practices of autonomous self-management. Beyond providing necessary services, these practices are geared towards freeing people from the necessity of waged labor, of valorization for capital. In this, self-valorizing activities challenge the limits even of the gift economy and shift emphasis again towards that great concern of anarcho-communists historically— the abolition of the wage system.

REFERENCES

Agamben, Giorgio. 1993. *The Coming Community*, trans. Michael Hardt. Minneapolis: University of Minnesota Press.

Bakunin, Michael. 1974. *Selected Writings*. New York: Grove.

Barbrook, Richard. 1998. "The High-Tech Gift Economy." *First Monday* 3(12): http://www.firstmonday.org/ojs/index.php/fm/article/view/631.

Barclay, Harold. 1990. *People Without Government: An Anthropology of Anarchy*. London: Kahn and Averill.

Benkler, Yochai. 2005. "Coase's Penguin, or, Linux and the Nature of the Firm." *CODE: Collaborative Ownership and the Digital Economy*, ed. Rishab Aiyer Ghosh, 169–206. Cambridge: MIT Press.

Benjamin, Walter. 1969. "The Work of Art in the Age of Mechanical Reproduction." In *Illuminations: Essays and Reflections*, ed. Hannah Arendt, 217–251. New York: Schocken Books.

Bey, Hakim. 1991. *Immediatism*. San Francisco: AK Press.

Bey, Hakim. 1996. *Millennium*. New York: Autonomedia.

Clastres, Pierre. 1989. *Society Against the State: Essays in Political Anthropology*. Boston: Zone Books.

Clastres, Pierre. 1994. *Archaeology of Violence*. New York: Semiotext(e).

Cleaver, Harry 1992a. "The Inversion of Class Perspective in Marxian Theory: From Valorization to Self-Valorization." In *Essays on Open Marxism*, eds. W. Bonefeld, R. Gunn, and K. Psychopedis, 106–144. London: Pluto.

Cleaver, Harry. 1992b. "Kropotkin, Self-valorization and the Crisis of Marxism." Conference paper, presented at conference on Pyotr Alexeevich Kropotkin, Russian Academy of Science, Moscow, St. Petersburg, and Dimitrov, December 8-14.

Clippinger, John and David Bollier. 2005. "A Renaissance of the Commons: How the New Sciences and Internet are Framing a New Global Identity and Order." In CODE, ed. Ghosh, 259–286.

Day, Richard. 2001. "Ethics, Affinity and the Coming Communities." *Philosophy and Social Criticism* 27(1): 21–38.

Del Re, Alisa. 1996. "Women and Welfare: Where is Jocasta?" In *Radical Thought in Italy: A Potential Politics*, ed. Paolo Virno and Michael Hardt, 99–113. Minneapolis: University of Minnesota Press.

Dolgoff, Sam. 1979. *The Relevance of Anarchism to Contemporary Society*. Minneapolis: Soil of Liberty.

Dolgoff, Sam. 1980. *The American Labor Movement: A New Beginning*. Champaign: Resurgence.

Dyer-Witheford, Nick. 2010. "Commonism." In *What Would it Mean to Win?* ed. Turbulence Collective, 105–112. Oakland: PM Press.

Ehrlich, Howard, ed. 1996. *Reinventing Anarchy, Again*. Oakland: AK Press.

Ehrlich, Howard, Carol Ehrlich, David DeLeon, and Glenda Morris. 1996. "Questions and Answers about Anarchism." In *Reinventing Anarchy, Again*, ed. Ehrlich, 4–18.

Esteva, Gustavo. 2010. "Enclosing the Enclosers." In *What Would it Mean to Win?* ed. Turbulence Collective, 23–29.

Free Association, The. 2010. "Worlds in Motion." In *What would it Mean to Win?* ed. Turbulence Collective, 98–104.

Ghosh, Rishab Aiyer. 2005a. "Why Collaboration is Important (Again)." In *CODE*, ed. Ghosh, 1–6.

Ghosh, Rishab Aiyer. 2005b."Creativity and Domains of

Collaboration." In CODE, ed. Ghosh, 7–12.

Ghosh, Rishab Aiyer. 2005c. "Mechanisms for Collaboration." In *CODE*, ed. Ghosh, 109–112.

Graeber, David. 2001. *Toward an Anthropological Theory of Value*. New York: Palgrave.

Graeber, David. 2004. *Fragments of an Anarchist Anthropology*. Chicago: Prickly Paradigm Press.

Hardt, Michael, 1996. "Introduction: Laboratory Italy." In *Radical Thought in Italy*, ed. Virno and Hardt, 1–10.

Hartung, Beth. 1983. "Anarchism and the Problem of Order." *Mid-American Review of Sociology* VIII(1): 83–101.

Holloway, John. 2010. "Hope Moves Faster than the Speed of Thought." In *What Would it Mean to Win?* ed. Turbulence Collective, 7–10.

Joll, James. 1964. *The Anarchists*. New York: Grosset and Dunlap.

Kropotkin, Peter. 1902. *Mutual Aid: A Factor in Evolution*. London: Heinemann.

Kropotkin, Peter. 1970. "Law and Authority." *Kropotkin's Revolutionary Pamphlets: A Collection of Writings by Peter Kropotkin*, ed. Roger N. Baldwin, 196–218. New York: Dover Publications.

Leach, James. 2005. "Modes of Creativity and the Register of Ownership." In *CODE*, ed. Ghosh, 29–44.

Mance, Euclides André. 2010. "Solidarity Economics." In *What Would it Mean to Win?* ed. Turbulence Collective, 66–73.

Marshall, Peter. 1992. *Demanding the Impossible: A History of Anarchism*. London: HarperCollins.

Mauss, Marcel. 1925. *The Gift: Forms and Function of Exchange in Archaic Societies*. London: Routledge.

Mezzadra, Sandro and Gigi Roggero. 2010. "Singularisation of the Common." In *What would it Mean to Win?* ed. Turbulence Collective, 30–36.

Proudhon, Pierre-Joseph. 1969. *Selected Writings of Pierre-Joseph Proudhon*. Garden City: Anchor Books.

Shantz, Jeff. 2009. "Re-building Infrastructures of Resistance." *Socialism and Democracy* 23(2): 102–109.

Shorthose, Jim. 2000. "Micro-Experiments in Alternatives." *Capital and Class* 72: 191–207.

Strathern, Marilyn. 2005. "Imagined Collectivities and Multiple Authorship." In *CODE*, ed. Ghosh, 13–28.

Vercellone, Carlo. 1996. "The Anomaly and Exemplariness of the Italian Welfare State." In *Radical Thought in Italy*, ed. Virno and Hardt, 1–10.

Ward, Colin. 1973. *Anarchy in Action*. New York: Harper Torchbooks.

Ward, Colin. 2004. *Anarchism: A Very Short Introduction*. Oxford: Oxford University Press.

Ward, Colin and David Goodway. 2003. *Talking Anarchy*. Nottingham: Five Leaves.

ABOUT THE AUTHOR

Jeff Shantz is an anarchist activist, poet, and sociologist, currently teaching critical criminology at Kwantlen Polytechnic University in Surrey, British Columbia. His books *Active Anarchy: Political Practice in Contemporary Movements* (Lexington, 2011) and *Constructive Anarchy: Building Infrastructures of Resistance* (Ashgate, 2010) offer autoethnographic analyses of anarchist participation within contemporary social movements. He is also the editor of the insurgent journal *Radical Criminology*.